HERE COMES HEAVEN

HERE COMES HEAVEN

A KID'S GUIDE TO GOD'S SUPERNATURAL POWER

MICHAEL SETH AND BILL JOHNSON

Cover Art and Illustrations by Tazia Hall.

Cover Design by Jennifer Neupauer.

DESTINY IMAGE® PUBLISHERS, INC.

P.O. Box 310, Shippensburg, PA 17257-0310

"Speaking to the Purposes of God for this Generation
and for the Generations to Come."

This book and all other Destiny Image, Revival Press, Mercy Place, Fresh Bread, Destiny Image Fiction, and Treasure House books are available at Christian bookstores and distributors worldwide.

For a U.S. bookstore nearest you, call
1-800-722-6774.

For more information on foreign distributors, call
717-532-3040.

Or reach us on the Internet:
www.destinyimage.com

ISBN 10: 0-7684-2502-6

ISBN 13: 978-0-7684-2502-4

For Worldwide Distribution, Printed in the U.S.A.

2 3 4 5 6 7 8 9 10 11 / 09 08

DEDICATIONS

To those who see children through the Father's eyes.

—Mike Seth

I dedicate this book to my grandchildren—Kennedy and Selah, Haley and Tea, Judah and Diego, and the two that are on the way—Braden and Isabella. May you always enjoy the adventure of bringing His world into ours.

—Bill Johnson

Acknowledgments

Bill Johnson—a true father who gave me an invitation to pursue my destiny and live a dream.

Bethel Church—an "Open Heaven" where advancing the Kingdom is not just an idea, but a reality.

Marilyn—Thank you for your support, encouragement, and ideas. You are a wonderful source of strength. I love you.

TABLE OF CONTENTS

Introduction

(A NOTE TO PARENTS AND MINISTERS.)

In the very early stages of "Renewal" at Bethel Church, Pastor Bill Johnson hired me as the children's pastor. As excited as I was to be a full-time minister to children, I, along with everyone else, was entering uncharted territory. I was being asked to lead a young generation in the realm of revival—without any blueprints, or framework to follow. One thing was for sure—life as we knew it was about to change.

After several weeks of earnestly seeking and praying for direction, I heard God's voice. He said, "I want to raise a prophetic generation." Wonderful! God spoke to me! But I had absolutely no clue what it meant!

Each week, church services at Bethel became encounters with God's manifest presence. Miracles, deliverances, and healings were witnessed along with laughter, "drunkenness" in the spirit, and other dignity-defying experiences of joy. These experiences were the result of Heaven depositing an amazing grace gift: an outpouring of the Father's love. Accompanying this "Open Heaven" phenomenon, were the incredible revelations of the Kingdom that pastor Bill Johnson would impart.

I now had a plan. And it was simple (it usually is when God is involved). I would begin to gather the deposits of heavenly activity and revelation and give it to our children. I felt the children deserved the same fresh "manna" that their parents were enjoying. As our young people began to encounter God's presence, the transformation was amazing. They learned to recognize and become intimate with the Father's love. They heard His voice, and discovered who they were.

As His children, they became confident. Our children began to prophesy, and lay hands on the sick as their hunger for Papa God increased. Each week we would hear testimonies of what God was doing through our children in their homes, schools, stores, and playgrounds. I am convinced that there are no truths or values of the Kingdom of God that cannot be received and carried by children. They were created for revival!

Wanting to "give away" what we were receiving, my wife, Marilyn, and I began to create teaching resources that captured Kingdom truths and principles. They were short, colorful, and easy to use. Over the past few years we have seen God use these materials in many nations, cultures, and generations. (Adults like them as well.)

It was an extreme honor when Pastor Bill Johnson invited me to co-author this work, to adapt his first book, *When Heaven Invades Earth*, for children. Bill's book has been aptly described as an invitation to walk and live in the miraculous power of God.

Throughout the pages the very heart and love of the Father is revealed, exposing the identity of those who call Him Lord. As His Royal Children, we are His heirs who receive an inheritance. This inheritance gives permission, equips, and releases us to pursue our destiny which causes Heaven to invade earth.

These truths have plucked the heart strings of Christians worldwide. There is a sincere desire and hunger for more—to live and demonstrate a true gospel of power. As Bill and his ministry team traveled, they heard frequent requests for such a children's book. It was a welcomed cry.

If we as fathers and mothers truly value this present outpouring of the Father's love and power, then we will not only want to preserve, but *advance* this move of God.

Gathering our inheritance which we enjoy and imparting it to our children is key to seeing global revival spread and increase. This truth terrifies the enemy and is the reason why he has done so much to devalue children.

Here Comes Heaven is a gathering of revelation. It exposes the Father's love, reveals children's identity, and describes their inheritance. It is also a vision and value statement of Papa God as He looks upon His "little ones." Within this context, children are invited on a journey to fulfill their destiny. During the journey, because of Whose they are, children will demonstrate the Kingdom of God and bring Heaven to earth!

But Jesus said, "Let the children alone and do not hinder them from coming to Me, for the kingdom of heaven belongs to such as these" (Matthew 19:14).

PART I

HERE COMES HEAVEN

CHAPTER 1

HEAVEN ON EARTH

A GOD STORY*

"Bungoma children for Jesus, Bungoma children for Jesus" was heard all over the city of Bungoma, in the country of Kenya in Africa. The streets were filled with over 2,000 children singing, dancing, marching, and carrying signs proclaiming, "Bungoma belongs to Jesus!"

Something huge was happening. Heaven "opened up," and wherever God's presence touched the town, miracles happened. The hospitals, prisons, businesses, and churches were all changing. The most amazing thing was the fact that God was using His children to bring Heaven to earth!

How did this happen? Just one year before this day of celebration, things in Bungoma were very different. Many of the pastors did not think that God could use children in a powerful way. They even thought children should wait until they grew up to get saved!

But, the Lord began to speak to the leaders about His children. God wanted His children to be seen and treated as valuable treasures. He wanted them to be raised up in His presence, love, and power. God had plans to use the "little ones" in a mighty way. The leaders obeyed and invited children's ministers to Bungoma. They gathered children from the churches, orphanages, and streets.

As the children received the Father's love and believed His word, they began to move in God's power, and many miracles happened. One group went to a hospital. The leaders told the children to just listen to the Lord and obey whatever Jesus said to do. The people in the hospital were sad, hurting, and sick. They were not really happy to see the children.

As the children prayed, one boy said, "I feel like God wants me to sing." As he raised his hands and sang a worship song, God's presence filled the room. The sick people were suddenly touched by God, and became hungry in their hearts for Him. They began to cry, and asked the children to come and help them receive Jesus. What an awesome day!

This made the children want to do even more with God. They didn't want to wait to grow up. God could use them right now!

The children started to pray for the entire city. Many people were led to the Lord and were healed in their bodies. More and more children came together, and soon there were prayer meetings taking place all over the city as the children prayed for God to do great things in Bungoma. This is when God gave them a plan.

THE PLAN

Bungoma was a city where the church leaders were not very close or friendly with each other. But the children didn't care. They liked each other and prayed together. They began to help and serve the pastors in the city. This touched the hearts of the leaders. They were sorry for their bad attitudes and asked for forgiveness. God began to heal the churches as the children led the way!

God wanted the children to march for seven days and have special meetings in the city. The day before the marches, the pastors met with the children. They asked the children to forgive them for not seeing them as God sees them, as valuable treasures who could know God and be used in a powerful way. They blessed the children and gave them a large key. This showed the children that the leaders honored them for having God's power and authority to do great things!

For the next seven days, the children shared God's love and power all over the city. Many people were saved, healed, and saw amazing miracles. In one hospital, over 100 people were healed in just one day, and they went home! Weeks later in another hospital, children were praying for people to be healed. So many people were healed before they were treated at the hospital that the hospital had to close down! To this day it is being used for business offices.

Each day the children led special meetings. It was powerful! The children preached, led worship, and touched many with God's power. More and more, pastors were seeing just how important and powerful children were, and how God wanted to work through them.

What happened during those seven days in August 2002 was just the beginning! All over the nation of Kenya, people continue to ask for the children to come and minister to them. Now, young people from other parts of Kenya want to do the same thing. The children of Bungoma still go to the orphanages, hand out food and clothes, and minister to the villages and hospitals. Leaders from schools, businesses, government, and even other religions have come together to honor and bless what the children have done.

Now, the pastors in the area have also come together to help the street children. Orphans without homes can now go to Christian homes where they will be taken care of and learn about God.

The children are now loved and valued in Bungoma. People have seen God's heart for them. He sees His children as mighty and powerful as they bring Heaven and the Kingdom of God to earth!

*Jennifer Toledo provided this amazing story. She was instrumental in training and leading the children who transformed Bungoma, Kenya.

JESUS LOVES CHILDREN

What an amazing and powerful story. Just think: children were powerful in God changed an entire city! You may never have heard a story like this before. But, do you know what? What these children did was normal in God's eyes. Showing God's love and doing powerful things, such as performing miracles, is normal.

Power happens when people find out who their Father is, and how much He loves them. Miracles happen when people discover they have His power and authority. Catching Heaven happens to people, especially young people, like you!

God doesn't want children to bring Heaven to earth only in Africa. He wants children all over the world to show His power, love, and glory. He wants you to show others what He can do. God loves you and sees you as a special treasure. He sees you doing mighty and powerful things for Him. He sees you changing the world!

This book, Here Comes Heaven, is an invitation. You are invited on a journey. It will be an exciting adventure that will continue for the rest of your life!

Your heavenly Father has much to show you about:

WHO HE IS.

HIS GREAT LOVE FOR YOU.

WHO YOU ARE.

WHAT YOU GET TO DO.

God has much to give you:

FOR YOUR JOURNEY.

FOR YOUR EXCITING ADVENTURE.

THAT WILL BRING HEAVEN TO EARTH!

CHAPTER 2

A ROYAL MISSION

Did you know Jesus could not heal the sick? He could not help people who were bothered by the devil, either. You might say, "No way, Jesus did all those things. The Bible says so!"

This is what Jesus said about Himself in John 5:19, "*I can do nothing.*" He did not bring any special powers with Him when He came to earth. Even though Jesus was 100 percent God, He chose to live on earth as a regular person just like you. Why would He do that?

Because He loves you.

Jesus did many miracles; but He did them *as a person* who was very close to His heavenly Father. If Jesus did all those miracles as God, then you could not do them, because you are just a person. But because Jesus *as a person* healed the sick, raised the dead, and helped people bothered by the devil, *then you can too!*

As a person, what was so special about Jesus?

HE HAD NO SIN, SO HE WAS
VERY CLOSE TO HIS HEAVENLY FATHER.

HE KNEW HE NEEDED HELP.

HE NEEDED THE SPECIAL POWER OF GOD—
THE HOLY SPIRIT.

So, what about you?

If you have Jesus in your heart, your sins have been forgiven. You are very close to Papa God. When Jesus died on the Cross, the power of sin was broken—*forever*! His blood has washed you and made your heart clean. When God looks at you, He actually sees His Son, Jesus. Nothing can keep you away from your heavenly Father—*nothing*!

And...you can have God's special power in your life.

A GREAT BATTLE

God had a plan for His Kingdom to cover the earth, but there was an enemy who wanted to stop Him from doing it.

Lucifer was the most beautiful angel God created. It was his job to lead all the worship in Heaven. The Bible says that thousands of angels and other creatures worship God at His throne. It sounds like a roaring waterfall! (See Revelation 19:6.) What an amazing sight and sound that must be!

There was such glory and celebration going on in Heaven, but then something very bad happened. Pride came into lucifer. He became jealous of God getting all the praise and worship. He thought he should be worshiped instead of God. Lucifer decided to take God's place on the throne. He gathered one-third of all the angels in Heaven, and led them into battle against God.

What do you think the battle was like? Was it like a terrible thunderstorm with loud crashing thunder, or maybe a big earthquake that shook everything?

Lucifer and his angels were beaten badly. They were cast out of Heaven and fell to earth, where they roam to this day. Lucifer's name was changed to satan, and his angels are known as demons.

In a split second, God could have destroyed the devil and his demons, but He chose to defeat darkness in the earth another way.

THE FATHER'S PLAN

When God created Adam and Eve, He put them in a very special place called the Garden of Eden. There was

no pain, sickness, or sadness in the Garden. There was nothing to be afraid of. It was full of joy, beauty, peace, and God's presence. It was just like Heaven on earth!

Adam and Eve were made in God's image. That means they could have fun with God, enjoy His love, and love Him. Adam and Eve also had a spirit in them that would never die. They could live with God forever and ever. Being made in God's image also meant that they were given authority. God gave them the power to rule over the earth. With this power and authority, God gave Adam and Eve something special to do—have children who would love Him. With this love, they would spread the heavenly Father's Kingdom of joy and peace all over the earth.

KEYS LOST

More than anything, satan wanted what Adam and Eve had—the "keys" of power and authority. If he had those keys, he could rule planet Earth, and everybody would have to worship him. How would satan do it? He could not invade the Garden of Eden and just take the keys. He had no power. The evil prince, satan, came up with a plan to trick Adam and Eve.

Satan came slithering into the Garden of Eden as a sneaky snake. He found Eve by the Tree of Knowledge of

Good and Evil. He lied to Eve and told her she would be like God and not die if she ate the fruit from the tree. God did not want Adam and Eve to eat of the Tree of Good and Evil. He loved them and only wanted them to know about His goodness and love. God wanted to protect them from knowing about evil things.

But Eve believed the snake's lie. She and Adam agreed with the devil, and disobeyed God. They ate the fruit. In one second it was done! Adam and Eve had given away the keys to the enemy. The devil now had the power to steal, kill, and destroy all that God had created on earth.

Because Adam and Eve chose to do wrong, they were now slaves. They would not rule over the earth. They would not spread God's Kingdom of love and goodness. Adam and Eve were under the authority and power of the devil. Sin now separated them from their Father. It was a terrible day.

Was everything lost? Was there any hope?

HELP IS ON THE WAY!

God's plan for people to rule over the earth did not end just because Adam and Eve sinned. His plan was to send His Son, Jesus. Jesus would take the punishment of sin. He would take back what Adam lost—the keys of power and authority. God the Father not only loved His

Son; He loved His children. He loves you. He was willing to let His own Son die so the children He loves could come to Him, and enjoy His love. It was the Father's plan of love.

Satan wanted to stop God's plan.

After Jesus was baptized in water and the Holy Spirit, He went into the desert. He wanted to spend time with His Father, and hear His voice.

That's when satan came to tempt Jesus. He said, "If you just bow down and worship me, I will give you those keys that you want" (Matt. 4:8-9, paraphrased).

But Jesus knew His Father's plan. He knew He was going to have to suffer and die to get the keys back. If Jesus would worship satan for just a few minutes, then He would not have to die on the Cross. Satan's idea might have sounded tempting, but Jesus said, "*No!*" (Matt. 4:10). He would not be tempted—he would obey and honor His Father. He would not honor satan's desire to be worshiped.

Father God's plan was for satan to be defeated by man—by someone who was made in His own image. Jesus would shed His blood and bring people back to the Father. When Jesus died on the Cross and was raised from the dead, satan was defeated. Jesus took back the keys of

power and authority. They are in His hands now. The devil lost again!

YOU WERE BORN TO RULE

When you asked Jesus into your heart, you were forgiven of your sins. You also received the reward of Jesus' victory over sin and death. You received the keys of power and authority. Jesus did all the hard work, but you get the prize—a free gift!

Do you want to hear the most amazing thing ever? *You* were born to be a ruler here on earth! You are a royal son or daughter of the King of the universe. Jesus said, "All authority has been given to me in Heaven and earth, and now it is all yours!" The Father's plan for people to rule and spread His Kingdom now includes you. No matter how young you may be, you are a Royal Ruler!

Even though satan was defeated and lost the keys, sin is still in the world. It is like a bad germ that has infected what God has made. Disease, sickness, poverty, fear, wars, and hate are here on earth because of sin. Being a Royal Ruler means you get to find and destroy these "germs." It is like breaking a chain that satan puts around people. The devil is still jealous of God, but he can never remove God from His throne. The only thing he can do now is try to hurt people. It breaks the Father's heart when people hurt.

Because you are one of God's royal children, you have been given treasures—His peace and goodness, His promises and love. You also have the power and authority to share these treasures with others, and change people's lives. Sickness, fear, and the evil things the devil does to people, will be broken and disappear. Amazing things will happen!

AN INVITATION

You are preparing for an awesome journey. You will discover what it means to be a prince or princess in your Father's Heavenly court. You will find out how special and valuable you are.

Like a royal knight, you have been given an important mission: to spread the Kingdom of God wherever you go, and bring Heaven to earth. All the Father wants is for you to love Him and be close to Him, just like Jesus was when He was on earth.

TIME WITH YOUR KING

As you come into God's presence, begin to think about what Jesus did for you.

He died on the Cross, and you have been forgiven of your sin.

Nothing can keep you from His love and presence.

Praise and thank Him.

Ask the Father to show you what He sees when He looks at you.

You are a Prince or Princess.

Look at the keys.

Have Him show you what your royal mission is.

He will be with you every step of the way.

JOURNAL TIME

Write about and draw what the Father sees when He looks at you.

_____

_____

_____

_____

_____

_____

_____

_____

_____

_____

What did He show you about your Royal Mission?

_____

_____

_____

_____

_____

_____

_____

Do you think you can do the same things Jesus did while He was on earth?

_____

_____

_____

_____

_____

JOURNEY ADVENTURES

Ask God to show you how you can give away your "treasures" to others.

Look for people who need God's kindness, peace, and love.

Ask someone who is sick if you can pray for them.

Write down what happened.

_____

_____

_____

_____

_____

_____

_____

CHAPTER 3

TURN AROUND AND SEE

Jesus was always full of surprises. Everyone thought He would come to earth as a king with a parade or marching bands like other kings. People expected Him to come with an army and powerful weapons and to rule over all the other kings. They thought, "At last, we will get even and destroy our enemies." Instead, He came as a little baby...*surprise!*

Oh yes, Jesus did come to destroy an enemy, a very bad enemy called sin, the devil, and all his evil deeds. But He had to do it according to God's plan.

The only ones who were not surprised by Jesus, were those who were hungry in their hearts for God. Stories had been told about a savior who was coming, and the hungry people believed the savior was Jesus. They didn't care if He didn't look like a king. They were still willing to change their lives and follow Him.

They saw Jesus as their Savior, their healer, and the One who would give them life. They believed Him when He said, *"The Kingdom of Heaven is at hand."* (See Matthew 4:17.) Jesus did not come to earth just as a poor baby born in a barn. He brought His world, the Kingdom of Heaven, with Him!

A TREASURE HUNT

When I was young, my friends and I played a game called "treasure hunt." Someone would hide the "treasure," usually a stick or a ball, out in a field. Then they would yell, "search!" The rest of us would begin to look for the treasure—backward. It was hard to look for something when walking backward, but that made it fun. There were times when the treasure was right next to me, but I couldn't see it. It would have been a lot easier if I was able to turn around and see the treasure.

In the same way, our "treasure"—God's Kingdom—is right here on earth beside us. Jesus said, *"Repent,* (stop walking backward and turn around), *because the Kingdom of Heaven is right here. It's right by your hand"* (Matt. 4:17).

You might ask, "Well, if God's Kingdom is right here, where is it? I can't see it!" God's Kingdom is all around you, *but*...it is an invisible world. You cannot see it with your eyeballs!

To *repent* really means to change the way you think about things. Things like who God is, and what He wants to do here on earth. When you begin to ask your heavenly Father to come and show you His love, and what Heaven is like, God gives you special "faith eyes." You will see His invisible world. It is amazing, but true! Sounds like a powerful gift, doesn't it? Jesus had this gift—it's called *faith*, and you can have it too!

"Seeing" God's Kingdom will help you feel just how close God really is to you. It is called His *presence*.

Your heavenly Father will show you through your "faith eyes" what you can't see with your eyeballs, like God's power to heal. It is more real and powerful than "seeing" someone who is sick. You will find out the things in God's world, like His peace, love, goodness, and kindness last forever. You will also find out that the things you can see in this world, like fighting, sadness, and anger, only last a short time.

HIDE AND SEEK

One of the most favorite things my sons enjoyed when they were young was to hunt for Easter eggs. My part in this game was to hide the eggs, just hard enough so the boys had to really look to find them. As they searched, I would walk with them and make sure all of the colored treasures were found. Sometimes I had to give them little hints. I was just as happy and excited as they were when each egg was found.

In Proverbs 25:2 it says, *"It is the glory of God to hide things, but is the glory of kings to find them"* (paraphrased). Does that mean your Father does not want you to know about Him and His Kingdom? No way! It is just the opposite. It is like those eggs I was hiding for my young sons. I hid them so they *could* be found! Some things are only discovered by a heart that really, *really* wants to know God. A hungry heart opens your faith eyes so you can see God and His world. Your Papa in Heaven gets so excited when you find the great treasures about Him and His Kingdom. He will help you find them!

THE KING'S KINGDOM

Do you know what a kingdom is? It is a place where a king is the ruler. It is where he is the lord and people obey his laws and authority. If a good king is the ruler, then all the people will be happy and have a good life.

Jesus came to give away all the good things of His world to those who would obey Him and be part of His Kingdom. He showed what those good things were when He forgave sinners, healed the sick, and set people free from the devil.

God's Kingdom happens when whatever is in Heaven comes down to earth. What is in Heaven? It is a place full of joy, healthy people, peace, and love. That is why Jesus taught His followers to pray, *"Your Kingdom come, Your will be done on earth as it is in Heaven"* (Matt. 6:10). Your Father wants you to enjoy and spread Heaven's good things wherever you go.

JESUS' GREATEST MESSAGE

While Jesus was on earth, people heard about Him and all the miracles that were happening. They came from near and far to see Jesus heal and to hear Him teach. They brought the sick, they brought people who were bothered by the devil, and those who could not walk. One day they saw Jesus heal all of them! What a sight to see hundreds of people healed and set free. How happy everyone must have been!

After these miracles, Jesus taught a great lesson. It was called the Sermon on the Mount. He started by saying, *"Blessed are the poor in spirit, for theirs is the Kingdom of Heaven"* (Matt. 5:3). Thousands of people were sitting along the hillside eager to hear what this amazing man had to say. They were wondering, "What does He mean by 'poor in spirit?'"

Jesus looked into the hearts of the people. They had walked for days following Him, leaving all they had behind, *just to be with Him.* They were poor in spirit—they were hungry for God. They wanted what Jesus had. Their hungry hearts brought the Kingdom of Heaven down to earth.

What was it about Jesus that made them so hungry? It was the presence of God, the Holy Spirit. The people could almost smell it!

What is your favorite food? Cookies? Cake? Pizza? When you begin to smell it cooking or baking, you start to get hungry. Soon, that favorite food is all you can think about. It is all you want, and you will stay close by, waiting for a bite.

Remember how hungry hearts for God open our faith eyes to see the Kingdom? Well, hunger for God's presence also changes our attitudes. An attitude is how you feel inside about something that makes you act a certain way. There are good attitudes and bad ones. Good attitudes are being helpful, kind, and patient. Bad attitudes are being selfish, rude, and cranky.

Hungry hearts of people also made them humble. They *needed* God. God really likes humble hearts. Humble hearts are hearts that can receive from God. It pleases our heavenly Father to give His Kingdom to those who are hungry.

The change in their attitude was like putting special glasses on their faith eyes. They could now see God's invisible world. When all this happened, Jesus started to talk about other attitudes that would help the people to see and enjoy even *more* of His Kingdom:

You will be so happy if you are humble [not full of pride], *for you will receive the earth* (Matthew 5:5, paraphrased).

You will be so happy if you are hungry and thirsty for God and what is right, for you will get filled up (Matthew 5:6, paraphrased).

You will be so happy if you show mercy [to those who need forgiveness, instead of being punished], *because you will get mercy when you need it* (Matthew 5:7, paraphrased).

You will be so happy if you are pure in heart [a heart that loves God and hates sin], *for you shall **see** God* (Matthew 5:8, paraphrased).

You will be so happy if you are a peacemaker, for you shall be called a son of God (Matthew 5:9, paraphrased).

You will be so happy even when people make fun of you for loving God and doing what is right, for you get to have the Kingdom of Heaven (Matthew 5:11, paraphrased).

Just look what you get with these good attitudes: God's Kingdom, mercy, happiness, seeing God, and much, much more! This is so important to know because many people think these are just a bunch of boring rules that you *have* to do. They are not rules, but ways to receive God's wonderful presents, called *blessings*!

Not only do we get those blessings, but God gives us another gift. It is the amazing gift of *grace*. God's grace helps us to not only live these attitudes, but *be* the *attitudes*! The Father wants us to become just like His Son, Jesus.

TWO KINGDOMS

The world that *cannot* be seen with your eyes is greater than what *can* be seen with your eyes. If people who follow God do not see and receive His Kingdom, guess what? There is another kingdom, the kingdom of darkness that tries to cause problems. The kingdom of darkness cannot be seen either until you see people who are sick, angry, poor, or afraid.

You don't have to worry or be afraid of this kingdom because here is some great news: Psalm 103:19 (AMP) says, "*God's Kingdom rules over all.*" *All* means everything! Aren't you glad?

Jesus said this in Matthew 12:28 (NIV), "*If I drive out demons by the Spirit of God, then the Kingdom of God has come upon you.*" Jesus only did miracles through God's power, the Holy Spirit (remember how good God's presence smells?), and the Kingdom of God comes when someone is set free from the devil.

It is like two worlds, or armies, in a battle—a world of darkness and a world of light. Guess which one will win every time? That's right! God's Kingdom of light is greater. Darkness always goes away when there is light!

When I was a teenager, a group of us went into a huge cave. There were many lights all along the path, and we were having so much fun. When we got to the deepest part of the cave, our guide had us stop. He reached over and turned off the lights. Wow! It was so dark! I could not even see my hand. You could almost *feel* the darkness. It was so strange, and kind of scary. We did not dare move! Then the guide lit one little match. It was like the sun had just entered the cave, and it felt so good to see again! He turned all the lights back on and the darkness was gone. We were able to continue to walk and not be afraid.

Faith is very important for you to be able to see how powerful the unseen world is. In the next chapter, you will find out how to use this gift of faith to bring God's Kingdom to earth.

TIME WITH YOUR KING

Your Father wants to show you His world, His invisible world. It's the Kingdom of God.

If you want to see it, you will. God will help you to repent, and change the way you think and look at things.

Ask your Heavenly Father to come right now. He will show Himself to you.

Even if your eyes are closed, you will see things.

YOU WILL SEE GOD.

YOU WILL EVEN SEE THINGS
THAT ARE IN HEAVEN.

YOUR HUNGER FOR GOD
WILL OPEN YOUR FAITH EYES.

Papa God really likes your hungry heart. You will discover great things about God and His Kingdom.

Ask the Father to help change your attitude.

He will.

Just receive, and thank Him.

Journal Time

Write about and draw what you "saw" when your eyes were closed.

_____

_____

_____

_____

_____

What did God show you?

_____

_____

_____

_____

_____

_____

_____

Did you see God?

_____

Did you see things in Heaven?

_____

_____

_____

_____

_____

_____

_____

Write what the Kingdom of God looks like.

_____

_____

_____

_____

_____

_____

_____

_____

_____

_____

_____

_____

_____

_____

JOURNEY ADVENTURES

When you go to school or play with your friends, is God showing you things?

_____

_____

_____

_____

If you saw a sick person, what did you "see"?

_____

_____

_____

_____

_____

How can you show God's love and goodness to someone who might be angry or sad?

_____

_____

_____

_____

Ask God to show you someone, and do it.

_____

_____

_____

_____

What happened?

_____

_____

_____

_____

Write down how God is changing your attitude.

_____

_____

_____

_____

_____

_____

_____

_____

_____

_____

_____

_____

_____

CHAPTER 4

FAITH—
THE EYES OF YOUR HEART

A GOD STORY

Some friends were visiting us one afternoon when we heard a knock on the door. It was a young mother who looked very worried. In her arms was her 6-month-old son. The baby was having a hard time breathing and was very upset. The mom was on her way to the hospital but wanted us to pray first. We gathered around them and began to pray. After a few minutes there was no change that we could see.

As she was about to leave, my son walked into the room, and we asked him to pray. As soon as he began to pray, we all felt something change in the room. My son continued to pray with power and authority out loud, but he was calm. When he was done, we opened our eyes, and what we saw was amazing. The baby was asleep, and breathing without any problem!

The happy mom took her son home and put him to bed. My son "saw" what was in Heaven, and his faith brought down healing and peace into our living room that day! He was only five years old.

As one of God's children you have been given a powerful gift. With this power, you will be able to see different worlds and different kingdoms that cannot be seen with your normal eyes. This gift is called *faith*.

Faith is like having eyes in your heart, or spirit. With these eyes you can see the invisible world. Many people think that this is just a special gift for only a few people. That is not true, because anybody can see!

You already have faith. It was by faith that you were saved, forgiven of sin, and became a Christian. By faith you believed, and received God's love, and asked His Son, Jesus, into your heart. (See Ephesians 2:8.) You did not see Jesus with your eyeballs, did you? But by faith you *know* for sure God is real, and you belong to Him.

Faith is what brought you into His family. It is how you came into His Kingdom. But you know what? That is not the end of it, it's just the *beginning*. Faith is how you get to see God's Kingdom and enjoy it every day!

WHAT THE BIBLE SAYS

In the Bible, there are some verses that really help you see with your faith eyes:

Matthew 6:33 (NKJV) says, *"Seek* [or look] *first the Kingdom of God...."*

In Colossians 3:2 (paraphrased) it says, *"Think on things that are above, and not on things that are on earth."*

The apostle Paul wrote, *"while we look not at the things which are seen, but at the things which are* **not** *seen; for the things which are seen are temporal* [temporary], *but the things which are* **not** *seen are eternal* [everlasting]" (2 Cor. 4:18).

God's Word is saying, come and look into a world that is invisible. That is what Jesus did. He did what He saw His Father doing first in Heaven. (See John 5:19.) Then He did it on earth. That's when miracles happened. That is when Heaven would come to earth. How did Jesus "see" His Father in Heaven? With His *faith eyes*!

LET'S GO TO SCHOOL!

The Father really wants you to see with your faith eyes. He even sent a teacher, the Holy Spirit, to help you. He will lead you and take you to places where you can learn. One of the greatest ways you can learn to see is

when you worship God. Your teacher, the Holy Spirit will lead you into the Kingdom of God, where true worship happens. You will "see" God's throne which is the center of His Kingdom. In that place, where you are loving and praising God, you will begin to see "unseen" things. God will show you what your mind, thoughts, and eyeballs might not understand, and that is all right. That is what happens when you are in God's presence.

One of the most famous people in the Bible is David. He killed lions, bears, and the huge giant, Goliath. He was even the king of Israel. But, do you know what the greatest thing about him was? David was a worshiper! His heart was close to the Father. He learned how to see God's Kingdom. He knew that God's presence was with him all the time. David saw God every day, with the eyes of faith because he worshiped God every day.

As you worship God, your faith eyes will open up more and more. You will see what your Father wants to show you.

SEEING THE UNSEEN

The invisible world is greater than the world you can see and touch. The more you know what God is really like, the bigger and stronger your faith will become. If you think that God sometimes puts sickness on people, how strong would your faith be?

Would you pray for a sick person to be healed? If you know that God heals, and gives only good things, then you can have faith for big things, like miracles. That kind of faith comes when you are close to Him, and when you know that He is a *good, good God!*

Do you know what the opposite of faith is? It's *unbelief.* Unbelief lives in the world that can be seen with your eyeballs. People who have unbelief trust what they see, feel, and hear more than in what their heart tells them. People who live by faith also know what they see, feel, and hear is real too. They just believe that the unseen world is *more* real.

If one day you go to school, to the store, or to the playground, and there is someone on crutches or in a wheelchair, what do you see? Unbelief sees someone who is hurt or crippled, maybe for the rest of their life. Unbelief says, "Oh, that is too bad." Unbelief may even feel sorry for that person, and walk away.

Faith sees something different, something not seen with your eyeballs. Faith sees what God sees—someone who could be healed by God's power if they were prayed for. Faith sees what is happening in Heaven before it happens here on earth. Faith sees that person running and jumping. Jesus did amazing miracles because He saw His

Father do it in Heaven first (see John 5:19). There is no sickness in Heaven, only healthy people, and that's just the way it should be here on earth! The Kingdom of Heaven (where you are *really* from) is greater and more powerful than what you see in this world.

"Ouch!" Your arm really hurts. If the doctor says it is broken, it would be silly to pretend it is not true. That is not faith. Real faith says, "Yes, it's true, I have a broken arm, but, what is *more* true is that Jesus took all my pain and sickness away 2,000 years ago (see 1 Peter 2:24). I can be healed!" There are no broken arms in Heaven, so your faith can bring healing down from Heaven to earth.

DON'T BE AFRAID

Have you ever had nightmares, or were afraid that something bad might happen tomorrow? That is called fear, and it is from the devil. Fear is having faith in the unseen world too, the kingdom of darkness. Fear comes when you believe something scary or bad is going to happen even before you see it. It also happens when you believe a lie that the devil may say to you, like "Your dog or cat is going to run away." When you start to think about it, and then believe it is true, you are agreeing with the devil and the lie. That is when fear comes into your heart.

How can you be safe from fear? Stay in God's presence. The closer you are to your Father, the more you will be covered and protected by His peace. It is just like a warm blanket. He will guard your heart and mind from fear. He promised! (See Philippians 4:7.)

Have other kids ever made fun of you because of what you said or did? It sure doesn't feel good, does it? Sometimes you might not say or do something because you are afraid of what they might think of you. That's when unbelief can happen.

You might be afraid that someone will make fun of you for having faith and believing God. They just don't know what you know about Him. It is much better to fear God than people. Does that mean you should be afraid of your heavenly Father? No way! It means to respect, trust, and obey Him. When you choose to believe that God is awesome and that nothing is impossible with Him, your faith will be strong. You won't be afraid of what other people may think about you.

IT'S IN THE HEART

Faith lives in your heart. God, the Holy Spirit, put it there. Faith is so much greater than what your mind thinks or knows. Faith is known within your *heart*—not your mind—that you believe God and are one of His children. Faith is so powerful because it is how you *agree with God*. Remember when Adam and Eve agreed with the devil? Something powerful happened, but it was very bad. When you agree by faith with God's thoughts, something powerful and *good* happens!

WALKING WITH A FRIEND

Your Father wants you to walk each day by faith, using your "heart eyes." The good news is that you won't be walking by yourself. You will be led by a wonderful friend, the Holy Spirit. He lives in your heart already. If you ask Him, He will tell you things, and will show you what to do and where to go. He will help you understand things. As you spend time with the Holy Spirit, you will know when He is talking to you.

FAITH—A PROMISE AND PROOF

Faith is a wonderful gift that sees into God's Kingdom. It also brings the things that are in Heaven down to earth. There is a very important verse in the Bible: "*Now faith is the substance of things hoped for, and the evidence of things not seen*" (Heb. 11:1 NKJV). Another way of saying it would be: Faith, or seeing with your heart eyes, is the *promise* of getting what you are hoping for, and the *proof* that you will get it before you see it with your eyeballs,

It works like this. Let's say you go to a place to eat with your parents, and they order a pizza. They pay for it, and they are given a number and a piece of paper (receipt) that shows that they paid for the pizza. As you sit down at a table and wait, you place the number on the table where the server can see it. That number is the *promise* that you will get what you are hoping for—the pizza.

If someone comes by and says, "Oh, your number isn't any good," your parents would show them the receipt that says they already paid for the pizza. The receipt is the *proof* that you will get what you ordered, even though the pizza has not been served yet. When the pizza is ready, the server looks for the number on the table and brings the pizza to you.

So how do you receive things from Heaven? God looks for your faith (just like the server looked for the number on your table), and then He blesses and gives you the good things He has in Heaven. Your Father honors and respects your faith. When you use your faith, it is like saying, "Papa, I trust and believe in you. Your Kingdom has all that I need."

Faith moves Heaven to earth.

HEROES OF FAITH

God's Word is full of amazing and exciting stories. Many heroes in those stories were just regular people who had faith and believed God.

By faith:

NOAH BUILT THE ARK (SEE GEN. 5-9).

ABRAHAM RECEIVED GOD'S PROMISES AND BECAME THE FATHER OF MANY NATIONS (SEE GEN. 12).

MOSES PARTED THE RED SEA (SEE GEN. 14).

DANIEL WAS PROTECTED IN THE LION'S DEN (SEE DAN. 16).

JOSHUA SAW THE WALLS OF JERICHO FALL (SEE JOSH. 6).

Great and amazing things happen when people use their faith. God is still looking for more heroes. *You* can be one too!

WHERE FAITH COMES FROM

So, where does faith come from? In Romans 10:17 it says, "*So faith comes by hearing, and hearing by the word of God.*" Not only does your heart have eyes, it has ears too! As you hear what the Father says to you each day, your faith and trust in Him will grow too. That's what happens when you spend time with your Papa God. It is so important to *read* God's word each day *and* to *hear* what He is saying all day long. Your Father is talking to you all the time. Just pick up the "faith phone" and listen!

FAITH IS LIKE A ROPE

When you use your faith, you please your heavenly Father! (See Hebrews 11:6.) Using your faith says you believe and trust God more than what you see happening here on earth. Faith knows that what is needed is already in Heaven, and just waiting to be given to you. Your faith is like a rope that can reach up to Heaven and bring down the answer.

Heaven hears your faith and answers back:

GOD WILL DO AMAZING THINGS.

MIRACLES WILL HAPPEN: BLIND PEOPLE WILL
SEE, AND CRIPPLED PEOPLE WILL WALK.

THE ENEMY WILL LOSE MORE
OF HIS KINGDOM.

THE KINGDOM OF HEAVEN
WILL COME TO EARTH.

A CHANGE INSIDE OUT

As you see more and more of what is in Heaven with your faith eyes, something will happen inside of you. You will have more courage. You won't be afraid to bring Heaven down to help people. You won't be shy when the Holy Spirit asks you to pray for someone. You will believe that *nothing* is impossible with God!

Read Matthew 9:20-22. This is a story about a woman who was sick for 12 years! You will read about how her faith gave her courage to touch Jesus. When she did, Heaven opened up, and she was healed.

You are a prince or princess, a royal son or daughter of the King. You have been given so much. You are a rich treasure to your Father. You also have the keys of authority and power to rule over the earth. Remember your royal mission? You are the one who can bring God's Kingdom of peace, healing, and joy to earth. Faith makes all this possible. How awesome is that?

In the next chapter, you will discover how to use your faith to bring lightning down from Heaven—with prayer.

TIME WITH YOUR KING

Welcome your friend the Holy Spirit. He lives within you always to give you power.

Ask Him to take you to your Father's throne in Heaven. He will do it.

See His throne.

Ask the Holy Spirit to lead you into worship.

Thank the Father for all He has done for you. See Him with your heart.

Tell the Father how much you love Him.

Come closer to His throne. Climb up on His lap.

Feel His love for you.

Let Him show you who He is and what He is like.

You will see that He is good. He has good gifts. Look at them.

Your faith will grow. You can believe that God will do amazing things for people.

JOURNAL TIME

Write or draw what the Holy Spirit showed you, and what you "saw" in Heaven.

_____

_____

_____

_____

_____

What did it feel like to be so close to Papa God?

_____

_____

_____

_____

_____

_____

Describe the Father's goodness, and His gifts.

_____

_____

_____

_____

_____

_____

JOURNEY ADVENTURES

As you set out on your daily mission, remember your friend, the Holy Spirit, is with you.

Listen to what He says. He will lead you and tell you when to use your faith.

Write or draw what you saw with the eyes of your faith.

_____

_____

_____

Was it different from what your eyeballs saw?

_____

_____

_____

_____

_____

_____

_____

Did your faith reach up to Heaven and bring down something that was needed on earth?

_____

_____

_____

_____

_____

_____

Write or draw what it was, and what happened.

_____

_____

_____

_____

_____

_____

_____

_____

CHAPTER 5

LIGHTNING FROM HEAVEN

A GOD STORY

It was on a Wednesday night at church. About 20 children showed up for our weekly Global Fire class. I had an idea what God wanted to do that night, but He did not tell me everything. He likes to surprise us.

I made a large circle of flags from different nations on the floor, and then gathered the boys and girls to sit inside. Tonight we were going find out what was on God's heart for the nations, and then pray what He showed us. What happened next was just amazing.

We started to worship and love on our heavenly Papa. It felt like Heaven "opened up," and God's presence filled the room. The children were now praying out loud, with all their heart and might. Soon, they were all laying face down on the floor, and some began to cry out for God to touch the people, to save and heal them. Then I took all the flags and covered the children with them.

As their prayers were getting stronger, my heart eyes opened, and I saw more than a thousand people being saved and set free from the devil! This went on for another half hour. By now, it was getting late, and parents were coming to pick up their children. As they walked in the room, the moms and dads fell backward and just sat down on the floor. God's presence in the room was powerful!

When I felt the Lord accomplished what He wanted to do, I asked the children what God had showed them. They all saw the same thing—large brick walls around cities and countries were breaking apart and falling down. People were running out from the walls laughing and singing. This was happening the same time I saw all those people getting touched by God and saved!

That night, the children came into God's presence. They "saw" His heart, and He showed them how to agree with Him and pray. They obeyed, and prayed. Heaven came down like lightning, and more than a thousand people came into the Kingdom of God.

Prayer is powerful!

JESUS SHOWS US HOW TO PRAY

In Matthew chapter 6, the followers of Jesus asked Him how they should pray. He taught them the "Lord's Prayer."

In this prayer, Jesus wanted to teach His disciples two really important things about prayer. First, when you worship God, you will become close to Him. Second, prayer brings Heaven to earth. When that happens, God's Kingdom comes and helps people.

As we get ready to look at this prayer, there is just one more thing to know. As one of God's children, you are really from another world. Your royal mission is on this planet, but earth is not your home. The reason you are here is to show God's love and power to others.

Let's take a close look at the Lord's Prayer and see what we can find. (See Matthew 6:9-13.)

OUR FATHER IN HEAVEN, HALLOWED BE YOUR NAME...

When you call God, "Father," it honors Him. It says what kind of special, loving relationship He has with you. Just think what God had to do to become your Daddy. He gave you all He had. He gave His Son and His love. Isn't He worthy for you to worship Him? The word *hallowed*

means "to respect and praise." Do you know what goes on in Heaven more than anything else? Worship and praise! Don't you think that should be happening here on earth, too? Worship is the most important thing you can do to honor and respect God. Why? Because God *lives* in your praise! (See Psalms 22:3.) God shows His power when you tell Him how great He is. It pleases Him so much, and He deserves it.

A 10-year-old boy named Dakota could not see very well. He had to wear thick glasses to help him see. One Sunday, during the worship service, his glasses began to get foggy, and he could not see. He took off his glasses. As he cleaned them, he saw a bright light. He put his glasses on, but he still could not see. He took off his glasses again, and looked around. He could now see perfectly! No one prayed for him. He was just worshiping, and God healed him!

Miracles like that are great, but should not surprise you. The Father always hears us, and He is moved by our praise and worship. Isaiah 42:12-13 says, "...*give glory to the Lord, and declare His praise...the Lord will go forth like a warrior. He will utter a shout...He shall prevail against His enemies.*" Just think: it's like when you praise and worship God, all of Heaven hears and answers you. The Lord rises from His royal throne. He puts on His battle armor and takes His sword. As if on a winged horse, He swoops down, finds the enemy, and fights the battle for you!

YOUR KINGDOM COME, YOUR WILL BE DONE ON EARTH AS IT IS IN HEAVEN...

Ready, aim, fire! This is the most important thing for all prayer. If the answer to the problem is in Heaven, then it should be let loose to come here on earth.

Let's say you see someone who is sick. Because you are close to God, He shows you His heart, and you are *ready*. He wants that person to be healed. Your faith "sees" the target. It sees that sickness being healed. Your *aim* of faith is steady on the target. Your prayer for healing is like *firing* and letting loose a lightning bolt from Heaven (with the answer to the problem). When that lightning bolt hits the target of sickness, what do you think is going to happen? Sickness disappears, and the person is healed.

What God wants is always happening in Heaven. It is His will for it to happen here on earth too. You can help bring Heaven to earth.

If something is not allowed in Heaven, then it must be bound or tied up here on earth. You can do that, too. Jesus said in Matthew 18:18, "*...whatever you bind on earth will be bound in Heaven, and whatever you loose on earth will be loosed in Heaven.*" When you pray like that, you are

using your keys of authority and power. All of the power in Heaven is yours to help you.

How much of Heaven should be here on earth? No one really knows, but the Bible says it is more than you can even dream or think about. Read Ephesians 3:20.

GIVE US THIS DAY OUR DAILY BREAD...

Is there anyone starving in Heaven? Of course not!

God's Kingdom on earth means that there is more than enough for what people need. God is a good Father who wants to give good things to His children. It makes Him happy to bless us, especially if we want to help others who are hungry and poor. Philippians 4:19 says, "*And my God shall supply all your needs from His riches in glory by Christ Jesus.*" This is God's promise, to give us all we need. He has lots of riches. Do you know where they are? In Heaven! Heaven is like a big house full of good things. We can receive them here and now!

AND FORGIVE US OUR DEBTS AS WE ALSO HAVE FORGIVEN OUR DEBTORS...

Is there any anger, fighting, or unforgiveness in Heaven? No way! It is a place of perfect peace and love. Heaven shows us how to treat others here on earth. The

Bible says in Ephesians 4:32, *"Be kind to one another, tenderhearted, forgiving each other, just as God in Christ has forgiven you."*

Do you know what a *debt* is? It is something you owe to someone. Your sin was too big a price to pay, but God forgave you because Jesus paid the price. Because you have been forgiven by God, you can forgive others who may have done something wrong to you. When you forgive a person, you are showing them God's love. This is what God's Kingdom looks like!

AND DO NOT LEAD US INTO TEMPTATION, BUT DELIVER US FROM EVIL...

There is no temptation or sin in Heaven, is there? You won't find anything evil there either. Staying far away from evil happens when you are in God's Kingdom. When He is close, sin and evil is far away.

James 1:13 says it is impossible for God to tempt you. That is what the devil does. This kind of prayer is important because it says you need *grace*. (Do you remember that grace is a gift that God gives to help you to do good things?) Your Father gives you grace to help you stay close to Him. This gift of grace will let you know that you need God's presence all the time!

When your heart is close to God, the devil is a big loser in your life. The Bible says in James 4:7, "*Submit* [give yourself] *therefore to God, resist,* [turn away from] *the devil, and he will flee from you* [take off running]."

When you are so close to your Papa God, you won't want to be tempted to sin. You won't even give the devil a chance. That is what this prayer is saying.

FOR YOURS IS THE KINGDOM, AND THE POWER, AND THE GLORY FOREVER. AMEN.

When you say these words in prayer, you are giving God praise. Your Father owns Heaven. That is why He can give you His Kingdom. All throughout the Bible you will find that God is being praised, and that "all glory and power is His." Your heavenly Father enjoys hearing it so much!

Do you want to hear a great idea? When you pray, spend most of the time just praising God. It is the most special thing you can do!

The Lord's Prayer shows us how to love and honor God by being close to Him in worship—bringing His Kingdom to earth.

A CLUE TO FINDING THE KINGDOM

*But seek **first** His kingdom and His righteousness, and all these things will be added to you* (Matthew 6:33, emphasis added).

In this Scripture verse, Jesus is giving a *big* clue to help Christians pray powerful prayers. He is saying seek (or find) His Kingdom *first*! Always ask God what He wants to happen *first*. Ask the Father what would please Him. What pleases the Father? To give us the good things from His Kingdom.

Why do you pray? God wants you to pray so other people will see Jesus and His Kingdom. When the Kingdom of God touches a person who has sin in their heart, that person is forgiven—there is no more sin. Hooray! When God's power meets sickness and disease, people are healed. Yeah God! When He finds those who are bothered by the devil, guess what? No more fear or bad thoughts. They are set free! When God's Kingdom rules on the earth, every part of a person can be healed—spirit, soul or mind, and body. Praise God!

When your faith eyes find God's Kingdom first, you will realize that Heaven is full and overflowing with everything that anyone needs.

87

SECRETS IN THE HEART

Have you ever seen a father holding his small child? Prayer can bring you that close to your heavenly Daddy. When God wants to tell you the secrets that are in His heart, He doesn't shout them out; He whispers. When you hear Papa's heart about something, just pray it. He loves to hear the echo of His heart when He hears you pray.

The power of prayer is amazing. It seems God is just waiting for His people to pray before He does something. He likes to answer your prayers! He has chosen to do His will and bring His Kingdom to earth through you. It comes through prayer.

What would happen if God's people didn't pray? The kingdom of darkness would rule over the earth. That is why the enemy is afraid of people who know how to pray, even children!

FROM ANOTHER WORLD

What country are you from? Where were you born? If you live there, then you are a citizen of that country. As a citizen, you will probably speak the language, wear the clothes, and eat the food from that country.

Paul said an amazing thing in Philippians 3:20, "*For our citizenship is in heaven, from which also we eagerly wait for a Savior, the Lord Jesus Christ.*" Paul was not talking about going to Heaven someday, but living as a citizen of Heaven *today*. That means as a child of God, you think, see things, talk, and act in a Heavenly way. Have you ever visited another country? What was it like? How did the people dress, talk, and live? Was it different? In the same way, you are visiting here on earth, but you are really a citizen in a different place. You are really from another world, God's Kingdom of Heaven!

Not only are you a citizen of Heaven, you are an ambassador of Heaven too. (See Second Corinthians 5:20.) An ambassador is a special person who represents his country while living in another country. As an ambassador, you represent, or show what Heaven is like here on earth.

An ambassador gets paid by the country he is from, not the country he is living in. As an ambassador of Heaven, you can have all the riches and good things that Heaven has. God said He would take care of you and meet all your needs. You do not have to worry!

If an ambassador is in danger, and might get hurt, the army from the country he is from will protect him. They are there to help him do his job. In the same way, God promises to protect you as His ambassador. He even has an army of angels ready to help you complete your royal mission!

You are from another world. You are what Heaven looks, talks, thinks, and acts like. You have Heaven's riches, God's love, and His presence. The keys of power and authority are yours. And now you know how to pray to bring His Kingdom to earth.

TIME WITH YOUR KING

Being in God's presence to worship Him is the first part of prayer.

Begin to praise your Father for what He has done for you.

Thank Him for all His good gifts.

Now just worship Him.

Tell him how great He is.

Tell Him how much you love Him.

Ask Him what is in His heart.

Be still, come closer to Him.

Listen for His whisper.

Listen for His heartbeat.

He will tell you, He will show you what to pray.

Begin to pray what you saw and heard from your Papa God.

Enjoy being this close to Him.

He will tell you how pleased He is with you.

Thank Him, and love on Him.

JOURNAL TIME

What did you hear when you listened to your Father's heart?

_____

_____

_____

_____

What did your faith eyes see when He showed you what to pray?

_____

_____

_____

_____

What did it feel like being so close to your Heavenly Father?

_____

_____

_____

_____

Write and draw what your heart heard and saw.

_____

_____

_____

_____

_____

JOURNEY ADVENTURES

How can you be an ambassador from Heaven?

_____

_____

_____

_____

Look for ways you can represent Heaven:

In your home

_____

_____

_____

_____

When you play

_____

_____

_____

_____

In your school

_____

_____

_____

_____

To someone who is sick, or sad

_____

_____

_____

_____

Write what happened when you were an ambassador.

_____

_____

_____

_____

_____

_____

_____

_____

_____

_____

_____

_____

_____

_____

CHAPTER 6

THE KINGDOM
AND THE SPIRIT

A GOD STORY

It was our first family mission trip. My wife, two sons (who were six and ten years of age at the time), and I were invited to Mexico. We were going to minister at a school that had several hundred children. We started by teaching about God, the Holy Spirit, and what He wants to do in our lives. It was exciting to see children being touched and blessed by God's presence. But it was only a hint of what the Holy Spirit wanted to do next.

After the first meeting, we were asked to visit the classrooms. As we walked into the first room of eight-year-old children, I felt the Holy Spirit come in with us. I told the children the Holy Spirit was with us and that He wanted to fill their hearts. I said that when the Holy Spirit comes to them, they will speak in a different language. That is how the Spirit praises God. They closed their eyes, and I prayed. As we touched each child, one by one they were filled with the Holy Spirit. God's presence was wonderful!

One boy, Roberto, was standing by himself in the corner of the room, watching. We were told that he was having had a hard time in school, and he was not very happy. As I walked toward Roberto, I felt I heard the Holy Spirit say, "When you touch Roberto, I will fill him with my presence."

I told the boy, "You are going to receive the Holy Spirit." I smiled and touched him. Roberto fell into a chair, and started speaking in another language.

In the next few minutes, all the children were on the floor, praising God in other languages (or "tongues" as the Bible calls it). As we left the class, I looked back and saw Roberto under his desk praising God with all his might. He had a huge smile on his face. We left to go to the next classroom, and the Holy Spirit went with us.

The Holy Spirit showed Himself that day in a very powerful way. God filled the children with Himself. It was the greatest gift He could have given them.

THE GREATEST PROPHET

Who is your favorite Bible character? Is it Noah, Moses, or a prophet like, Daniel or Elijah? Do you know who Jesus thought was the greatest? John the Baptist. John didn't do any amazing miracles, but Jesus said he was the greatest of *all* the prophets.

Who was John?

John was Jesus' cousin. People thought he was a bit strange. He lived in the desert, wore animal skins, and ate bugs! As a prophet, he baptized people. He told them to repent and get ready for the Lamb of God who would take away the sin of the world (see Matt. 3:2). The Holy Spirit told John that his cousin, Jesus, was the Savior. John said, *"...He who is coming after me is mightier than I...He will baptize you with the Holy Spirit and fire* [power]" (Matt. 3:11).

One day Jesus went to the River Jordan where John was baptizing people. Jesus walked into the water and asked John to baptize Him. John said, "No, I need to be baptized by *you*" (see Matt, 3:13-14, emphasis added). But John obeyed Jesus and baptized Him.

An amazing thing happened as Jesus came up from the water. Heaven opened up, and God (the Holy Spirit) came down upon Jesus like a gentle dove. At that moment, the heavenly Father spoke in a loud voice and said, *"This is my beloved Son, in whom I am well pleased"*

(Matt. 3:17). Now the Holy Spirit was upon Jesus—giving Him all the power He needed to change the world!

John knew that He needed what Jesus had—the baptism of the Holy Spirit and power. He knew that Jesus was the Savior of the world, and he knew how important the Holy Spirit was to bringing Heaven to earth. That is what made John the greatest of all prophets.

Do you want to hear something amazing? Jesus said that the least known of all people in the Kingdom of God is greater than John the Baptist! (See Matthew 11:11.) What did He mean by that? Jesus was saying that He was going to give something that no other Bible prophet or king ever had. This gift would be given to any person, great or small, who asked for it. This gift is the Baptism of the Holy Spirit. God wants everyone to have it.

TWO REASONS

Did you know that Jesus came to earth for two reasons? Both were very important. The first one was to pay the price for our sin so everyone could be forgiven and become a Christian. The second reason was so every Christian could be filled with the Holy Spirit. God wants every person to be filled and to overflow with...*Himself!* The Bible says it this way, "...*that you may be filled with all the fullness of God*" (Eph. 3:19).

A NEW LANGUAGE

When people were filled, or baptized in the Holy Spirit, amazing things happened. Miracles took place, God's power was shown, and people spoke in different languages (or tongues). Speaking in tongues is a language that your spirit uses to speak to God. It is a language that your mind does not understand, but that's okay. You don't have to know. Praising God in this different language blesses God, and tells Him how great He is (see Acts 2:11). It makes Him feel great! Speaking in tongues blesses you, too. The Bible says in Jude verse 20, that praying in the Holy Spirit, or tongues, makes your spirit strong. It is like taking spiritual vitamins!

Many people think that speaking in tongues is all that happens when they get filled with the Holy Spirit. But there is more, a lot more!

THE POWER OF THE HOLY SPIRIT

Jesus did not perform any miracle, heal any sick body, or set anyone free from the devil, until He was baptized in the Holy Spirit. He needed God's power to do what the Father asked of Him. You need the same power to do what your Father asks of you—to complete your royal mission.

It is the power of the Holy Spirit in a person that makes God's Kingdom of light chase away the kingdom of darkness. When that happens, people are set free from the darkness of sin, sickness, sadness, and anger. Darkness always leaves when a light is turned on. The kingdom of darkness always goes away when God's light of healing, joy, and love comes. Just as a light bulb needs power to shine, so does God's light—the Holy Spirit is the power.

THE PRESENCE OF THE HOLY SPIRIT

Your Father is such a good God! He has so many wonderful gifts for you. But do you know what the greatest gift is? The Holy Spirit Himself! Having the Holy Spirit *in* you means you can be so very close to God.

When people in the Old Testament heard God's promise of, "...the Lord your God is with you wherever you go" (see Joshua 1:9), they were able to do amazing things:

MOSES BROUGHT THE ISRAELITES OUT OF EGYPT.

JOSHUA LED THE ISRAELITES INTO THE PROMISED LAND.

GIDEON BECAME A BRAVE WARRIOR.

When Jesus told His disciples to, "Go...and preach the gospel to all nations..." (see Matt. 28:19). He told them that He would be always with them.

It is God's presence that makes impossible things, possible. He will make your royal mission possible, too. It is His promise to us.

The presence of the Holy Spirit shows people what God's Kingdom is really like. Peter had the presence of the Holy Spirit and people were healed just because he walked by them. It wasn't Peter's shadow that healed people; it was the shadow of the Holy Spirit. (See Acts 5:15.) Jesus had the presence of the Holy Spirit, too. Anyone who touched His clothes was healed. (See Mark 6:56.)

Follow the Leader

I liked to play "Follow the Leader" when I was young. One person was chosen to be the "Leader," and the rest of us would have to follow wherever the leader went. The game was fun because we did not know where we were going or where we would end up. Only the leader knew. It was always an adventure as we followed the leader over rocks, under bushes, and around trees. The fun was in the following.

That is the way it is with your Friend and Leader, the Holy Spirit. He knows where to go and what to do. He may want you to pray for someone, or do something strange that you may not understand. Just trust Him and obey what He asks. That is what makes being a Christian fun and exciting—just follow the Leader! That is what happens when you are baptized in the Holy Spirit. That is the way Jesus lived on earth. His life was pretty exciting, too!

FILLED AND REFILLED

Can you be baptized in the Holy Spirit only once? *No!* The Bible says that the followers of Jesus were filled with the Holy Spirit (see Acts chapter 2), but they were also filled *again* (see Acts chapter 8).

Why? Does the Holy Spirit leak out? The answer is yes!

Just like a plant needs water to grow and be healthy, you a need a fresh "drink" of the Holy Spirit. If you played or worked hard outside, wouldn't you get hot and thirsty? You need to be refreshed. If you pray for people and give away God's love to others, then you need to get filled up again. You cannot give away something if you are empty. Besides it is *fun* to get more and more of God's presence and "soak" in His love. He really enjoys pouring out His Spirit on His children!

So...get filled and refilled with the Holy Spirit every day!

TIME WITH YOUR KING

Jesus wants you to have everything He has...*everything*!

He even wants you to have His very Spirit, His own presence.

Close your eyes and invite God's presence.

Ask Him to fill you with His Holy Spirit.

He is a free gift; He will come to you.

Let Him fill you up...so much that you feel like He is overflowing in you.

Feel His presence in you...welcome Him.

Feel His joy...thank Him.

Let your spirit, not your mind, thank Him.

Let your heart tell Him how great and wonderful He is.

It's OK if you don't understand the words you are speaking.

It's called speaking in tongues.

Your heart knows. God knows. He understands your words...and He is pleased!

Enjoy what is happening.

This is only the beginning. Speaking in tongues can be a big part of your friendship with God. Your heart wants to talk to God in tongues all the time.

Practice, practice, practice every day.

JOURNAL TIME

After you have enjoyed this time with the Holy Spirit, write or draw what it was like to be filled to overflowing.

_____

_____

_____

_____

_____

How did it feel to be so close to God?

_____

_____

_____

_____

_____

_____

How did your heavenly Father feel about this time with you?

_____

_____

_____

_____

_____

JOURNEY ADVENTURES

Now that you have experienced the Holy Spirit this way, do you feel like you have more courage?

_____

_____

_____

_____

Do you feel like you are not alone, but have God's presence and strength in you?

_____

_____

_____

_____

Do you feel you can do things that you were afraid to do before?

_____

_____

_____

_____

_____

_____

_____

Share what happened with your parents and friends.

_____

_____

_____

_____

_____

_____

_____

_____

Write down how things seem different now. Write the things that the Holy Spirit is saying to you.

_____

_____

_____

_____

_____

_____

_____

_____

_____

_____

_____

_____

_____

_____

CHAPTER 7

SMEARED WITH GOD

A GOD STORY

The junior high youth group went to an amusement park just to have fun for the day. For the first two hours they were having a great time going on rides. Then, two boys saw a man with a cast on his arm. They started to talk to him. The man said he hurt his arm while working, and he was in a lot of pain. The boys prayed, and after a few seconds they told him to see if the arm was better. The man started to move and bend it. "Oh my gosh!" he shouted, "It's all better!" His wife was so happy she started clapping. Now the boys saw people who needed prayer everywhere.

After a few more miracles, the excited boys met the rest of the group and told them what God had done. They asked the group if they wanted to see miracles today. After they said yes, the two boys put their hands on the teenagers and prayed for them. Then they all went to pray for people in the park.

The young people said when the two boys prayed for them, they felt courage, and were not afraid. By the end of the day, the youth saw amazing miracles. Several people who were in wheelchairs got up and walked without pain! God used the youth group in a great way that day.

Those two boys gave to their friends what they had. It was God's power and the anointing of the Holy Spirit.

POWER FOR THE PLAN

The heavenly Father gave His Son a royal mission. Jesus would make a way for all people to come to the Father. He was also going to show the world who the Father really was by showing what Heaven was like.

This could only be done if Jesus was able to do powerful things like miracles. He was going to need power to do them. He needed God, the Holy Spirit. Jesus not only needed the Holy Spirit in Him, He needed the Holy Spirit on Him. When the Holy Spirit comes out, or on a

person, we say that person is "anointed." The word *anoint* actually means "to smear, or cover."

In Bible days, when someone was going to become a king or prophet, they would be anointed with oil. Oil was poured out and smeared all over the person to show that they were ready to be a king or prophet.

JESUS, THE ANOINTED ONE

The very name, *Jesus Christ*, means "Jesus, the anointed one." It was this anointed power that helped Jesus do what He saw His Father doing in Heaven. It was this anointing that caused all of those powerful miracles. People "saw" and "smelled" the Holy Spirit and power on Jesus. That is what they wanted. That is why they left everything behind to follow Him.

This powerful anointing scares the devil and his kingdom of darkness. He will do anything he can to stop the anointing. He tried when Jesus was on earth, and that is why the religious leaders had Jesus put to death.

The devil doesn't care if people think Jesus was just a teacher or a good man who tried to help people. But he does care about and is afraid of God's power. Even today he tells people, "Oh, those miracles that Jesus did were only for Bible times, and not for today." Or he'll say, "It is

the devil who did those miracles you hear about today."
Now, that is just silly, isn't it?

The enemy is afraid of God's power because it is the
anointing that breaks the chains of sickness, fear, and
anger that the devil puts on people. He loses! It is the
anointing, or what the Holy Spirit does, that invites people to enter God's Kingdom.

If Jesus needed the anointing of the Holy Spirit, don't
you think you need it too?

Jesus Sends the Holy Spirit

One day, Jesus told His disciples it would be better for
them if He went back to Heaven (see John 16:7). The disciples were confused. How could going away be a good
thing? By going back to Heaven, Jesus was able to send
the Holy Spirit to all of His followers, no matter where
they were in the world.

The Book of Acts is full of exciting stories about how
Jesus' disciples were "filled" and "full" of the Holy Spirit.
People were healed, raised from the dead, and set free
from being bothered by the devil. It happened every time
God's power was shown—every time!

The Holy Spirit lives in your "house" or spirit. When
He's in your "house," you will enjoy His presence and

closeness. It is so great when you get filled up with His power.

LIKE A GLOVE

My dad loved to make vegetable gardens. When I was old enough, I would help him by digging up the ground with his big shovel. Before long, I would get blisters on my hands, big ones, and I had to quit. Oh, did they hurt! Then one day, my dad gave me some gloves. It made a huge difference! Then I was able to dig and dig, and I didn't get any blisters!

The anointing of the Holy Spirit is like those gloves I put on to cover my hands. It makes the impossible, possible. The awesome, powerful things God wants to do with you, like healings and miracles, are impossible to do by yourself. That is why the anointing of God's Spirit comes. The "gloves" are put on so you can do the impossible. When that happens, Heaven comes to earth.

LEAKING THE HOLY SPIRIT

So, how does the Holy Spirit "leak out" of you to do powerful things? Is the Holy Spirit just a boss who makes you do whatever He wants? No way! The Holy Spirit is a person and wants to be with you. Isn't it more fun and exciting to do things with your friends than just by yourself? He wants to be friends and "team up" with you as a partner. He won't force you to do great things. He will invite you. Just say *yes*!

The Holy Spirit "leaks out" when:

- You know His presence is in you. Getting filled up with Him over and over again is really good. (See "Time With Your King" at the end of this chapter.)

- You have God's compassion for people. Compassion is more than just feeling sorry for someone who is sick, or needs help. It is a powerful force that loves people and hates what the devil did to them. Compassion is what moved Jesus, and released the anointing for Him to heal the sick and set people free from the devil.

- You are willing to do what the Holy Spirit asks you to do. Maybe He will want you to pray for an older person who is sick, or a friend at school who is having problems. Obey Him, and don't be afraid. He'll be the glove, and you won't get blisters!

- You let the Father use you to do impossible things, like miracles. See His power change things, and watch His Kingdom come.

This is what makes your royal mission so exciting, and possible!

GOD'S WORD, GOD'S VOICE

Did you know God is speaking to you all the time? He also likes to use different languages. Do you think one language is more important than another? No! If they are from God, then they are all important! Two languages He uses a lot are His Word (the Bible), and the quiet voice of His Holy Spirit. Both are needed.

Knowing God's voice happens when you spend time with Him, trust Him, and depend on Him. Like a friend who calls you a lot, you know the sound of their voice. The Bible is the Word of God. He wants you to know what is in His Book. God's voice that you hear in your heart will always agree with His Word. That same voice will help you understand the Bible.

Your Father is pouring out His Spirit and His presence more and more. It is like rain from Heaven. The more you get "soaked" and filled up, the more you will know His voice.

TIME WITH YOUR KING

As you invite the Holy Spirit to come, let Him "soak" and "fill" you with Himself.

It will refresh and make you feel alive inside.

It's like you are a plant that just had a drink of fresh water.

Feel His joy, it will give you strength.

Hear what He says to you.

You'll know that anything the Spirit asks you to do is possible.

Thank Him for His love, presence, and power that you have been given.

JOURNAL TIME

Write down the things you are learning about the Holy Spirit.

_____

_____

_____

_____

_____

What does He look, sound, and feel like?

_____

_____

_____

_____

What does it feel like when He comes to fill you up?

_____

_____

_____

_____

_____

_____

_____

Can you trust Him to lead you each day?

_____

_____

_____

_____

_____

_____

_____

_____

Did He show you something to do, like pray for someone?

_____

_____

_____

_____

_____

_____

Write what the Holy Spirit wants you to do today.

_____

_____

_____

_____

_____

_____

_____

_____

Write what happened when you did it.

_____

_____

_____

_____

_____

_____

_____

It is so much fun to write what God is doing through you! Write what you are feeling.

_____

_____

_____

_____

_____

_____

_____

_____

JOURNEY ADVENTURES

The Holy Spirit is *in* you for you to enjoy. The Holy Spirit is *on* you for others.

Look for those who need to see and feel God's presence and power.

Be willing to let God use you.

Ask your friend and partner, the Holy Spirit, what He wants you to do.

Let His compassion move you.

Let the "glove" give you power to do the impossible.

Write about when the Holy Spirit "leaked" out of you.

_____

_____

_____

_____

HERE COMES HEAVEN

PART II

HEAVEN ON EARTH

CHAPTER 8

SHOW AND TELL

A GOD STORY

It was getting late. The big room upstairs at church was filled with more than 100 children. God had done amazing things all week. The children learned how to heal the sick, pray, and prophesy over people. We were now going to show a video and have everyone rest. As we were trying to get the television to work, my wife whispered to me that a girl in our group was healed earlier that day. I thought, "Hmm, let's share some testimonies until the video is ready."

Just then, I felt the Holy Spirit say, "Teach about words of knowledge."

I obeyed, and taught for five minutes about this gift of the Holy Spirit. The Holy Spirit then said, "Now, let's show them how to do it."

I had the children close their eyes and ask the Holy Spirit for words of knowledge. After we prayed, I asked, "Who has a word?" About 12 hands shot up into the air. One by one the children came up and told us where they had a pain or a feeling in their body. (That is one way God gives a word of knowledge.) We then asked who in the room had that kind of pain. When a child raised their hand, we would pray for healing to come, and for the pain to leave. It was amazing! *Every* child who was prayed for was healed!

About 45 minutes later, I said, "Wow! There must have been 30 children who were healed tonight! Isn't God awesome?" An 8-year-old boy raised his hand and said, "There were actually 35 children who were healed. I wrote about each one in my journal."

The children learned about words of knowledge that night because they heard God's voice, saw His power, and felt His healing touch.

SHOW AND TELL

One of my favorite things about school was when we got to do something called "Show and Tell." We would have to find something from home and bring it to class to show and tell about it. The item might have been an object from a different country, a toy, or even something we never saw before. The best part about Show and Tell was not just telling about the object, but showing everybody something we could see, touch, or sometimes even taste! It was a fun way to learn.

Did you know that is how Jesus taught about the Kingdom of God? He liked Show and Tell, too! Whenever Jesus told people about His Father, and what Heaven is like, He also showed them powerful things like miracles.

THE BIBLE SAYS...

*And Jesus went to the churches and taught about the Kingdom **and** healed all kinds of sicknesses and diseases"* (Matthew 4:23, paraphrased).

*Then Jesus went to the cities and churches teaching and telling people about the Kingdom **and** healing every sickness and every disease* (Matthew 9:35, paraphrased).

*Later, Jesus would say to His disciples, "Go, and tell everyone the Kingdom of Heaven is at hand, **and*** *then heal the sick, raise the dead, and set people free from the devil"* (Matthew 10:7-8, paraphrased).

Jesus was never boring. He didn't want to just *tell* people about the Kingdom of God, He wanted to *show* them what the Kingdom was like, too. When the people heard Jesus teach, and then saw Him do miracles, they understood what He was saying to them.

HIS PRESENCE AND POWER

The Kingdom of God is all about God's presence being seen and felt. It is also about God's power. That is why Jesus had to show the presence and power of the Holy Spirit. Presence and power means miracles. Heaven is ready to show what the Kingdom is like whenever you tell someone about it. It is like being on a team where each person does his part to win.

DON'T BE A BALLOON HEAD

What happens if people just *hear* about God's Kingdom and don't see His presence and power? They will never really see the Kingdom of God. They will also turn into balloon heads! The apostle Paul said they would be "puffed up" with knowledge (see First Corinthians

8:1). Pride can fill our hearts and minds if Bible stories are all we know.

God's Word, the Bible, is an amazing book. It tells us so much about God, His love, and His Kingdom. It has lots of good stories, and they are all true. Our Heavenly Father wants us to study and know what it says...*but* just knowing the Bible, its stories and memory verses is not enough. Even the devil knows Bible verses!

In First Corinthians 4:20 it says, "*The Kingdom is not just words, but power.*" It is God's presence and power that show what the Word of God says. That is what makes God's Word alive, and feeds your heart. Big hearts are much better than big heads!

KNOWING GOD

Do you have a hero? Do you know someone who is special? How did you get to know that person? Did you read a book, or hear someone talk about that person? How much better would it be if you could meet that person, or even live with them? Wouldn't it be fun to go places and do things together? Then, you would *really* get to know them, right? Well, that is the way it is with God. Being a Christian is not just a good idea. It is all about being very close to a person...Papa God.

Just like a book about a famous person, the Bible tells about God and what He is like. But that is just the beginning. It is God's Spirit and power that allow you meet Him and learn about His Kingdom. What is even better, you get to live with Him and be in His Kingdom! How great is that?

How does all this happen? Remember when the people heard about Jesus and then saw what He did? Miracles and healings were happening everywhere! The Holy Spirit was on Jesus, and they saw His power. That made the people so hungry that they followed Him. They met Jesus because they could see, feel, and "smell" the Kingdom of God.

People don't want to just know *about* God. When they see God and His power, people's lives can change.

A MAP OR A GUIDE?

Discovering God's Kingdom is like going on a treasure hunt adventure. "Treasure Map" was a fun game we would play when I was young. Sometimes, though, it was hard to read the map and clues, and understand what they meant. When that happened, I could not find the treasure, and one time I even got lost! It would have been a lot easier if I had someone to guide me and help me understand the clues that were on the map. I would have found the treasure for sure.

God's Word is like a treasure map that has all the clues about God and His Kingdom. But God also has a guide for you—the Holy Spirit. Only He can help you understand the "clues" in the Bible. When you ask Him to help you, it makes your Heavenly Father very happy. He will see your hungry heart. Remember the verse, "*It is the glory of God to hide things, but it is the glory of kings to find them?*" (Prov. 25:2, paraphrased). The Holy Spirit will help you find those good things. When you read God's Word, He will feed your hungry heart. The strange thing is, the more the Holy Spirit feeds you from God's Word, the hungrier you will get!

Because God loves you so much He will give you a Guide, not just a map. Your Guide, the Holy Spirit, will lead you, show you, and give you power to be and do what His Word says.

GOD'S LOVE LETTER

When the Holy Spirit is invited, God's Word will bring you closer to Jesus. You will feel like you need Him more and more. You will want to know Him and His power. When you read the Bible, it will be like reading a love letter from someone who is very, very special to you.

You will be able to do what Jesus did—tell others about the Kingdom of God, and then show it wherever you go.

TIME WITH YOUR KING

Take your Bible and find a quiet place.

Ask the Holy Spirit to take you into Father's presence.

Thank your Papa for His love and goodness.

Tell Him how great He is and worship Him.

Let Him love on you, and enjoy being so close to Him.

Now ask the Holy Spirit to show you things from God's Word.

Open your Bible to Matthew, Mark, Luke, or John.

Read about what Jesus said and did.

Let the Holy Spirit feed and bring your heart closer to Jesus.

Read some more.

Take your time and see what Jesus wants to do.

Thank Him for this time.

JOURNAL TIME

Write what the Holy Spirit showed you in God's Word.

_____

_____

_____

_____

What did your hear?

_____

_____

_____

_____

_____

What did you see? Draw a picture.

_____

_____

_____

_____

What did you feel when you were getting closer to Jesus?

_____

_____

_____

_____

_____

_____

Did reading God's Word seem different this time? How?

_____

_____

_____

_____

_____

_____

JOURNEY ADVENTURES

Ask the Holy Spirit to show you someone who needs to know about the Kingdom of God.

The person may be at home, school, the playground, or the store.

He will show you someone.

Tell that person about God's love and power. The Holy Spirit will be there with you.

Ask the person if you can pray for them.

Invite the Holy Spirit to fill them with God's love.

If the person has any pain, ask if you can pray for them.

After you pray, ask how they are feeling.

As they feel better, let them know it is God's power and love that they are feeling.

Write what happened.

CHAPTER 9

THE WORKS OF THE FATHER

For hundreds of years, prophets (those who could hear God's voice) told people that a King would be coming to save them. They gave over 300 hints about who the Savior was going to be. The prophets even said when He would come and what He would do.

The night Jesus was born, all Heaven exploded with joy and celebration. Angels appeared and told the news of His birth, *"For there is born to you this day...a Savior, who is Christ the Lord"* (Luke 2:11 NKJV). Even a great star was placed in the night sky to guide the wise men to Jesus.

People were excited when they heard all the great hints about a Savior who would set people free from the devil. Jesus came to earth because He had a royal mission that would change the whole world. Even though Jesus was the most important person ever to walk on earth, He said an amazing thing, *"If I do not do the works of my Father, do not believe me"* (John 10:37). How could Jesus prove who He really was? *Miracles!*

THE FATHER'S BUSINESS

Just like many children, Jesus grew up with an earthly mom and dad. He did His chores every day and helped His dad in the carpenter's shop. He learned to read and write, and played games with His friends. Even while all the normal things were happening, Jesus was finding out who He was, and why He came to earth. He was here on a mission—to do the Father's business.

A GOOD SON

His parents, Mary and Joseph, were upset and afraid when they could not find Jesus. Where was He? He was only 12 years of age and nowhere to be found! He was separated from His mom and dad on their way back from a trip. Was He left behind? Is He okay? Finally, they found their son in the temple. Jesus was talking to and teaching the priests and religious leaders! Jesus was not sorry when He saw His parents, who were a bit confused. All He said was, *"...Did you not know that I must be about my Father's business?"* (Luke 2:49).

Even though Jesus was a good son to His earthly parents, He was first of all the Son of God. He was here to do the works of the Father, and destroy the works of the devil. That was the Father's business.

A RIGHT HEART

Because Jesus had a pure and obedient heart, His plan to do the will of the Father was simple. He would follow and do what His Father was doing in Heaven. Jesus said, *"Whatever I see the Father do, that is what I will do"* (see John 5:19a). He also said, *"I only say the things I hear from my Father"* (see John 8:26).

Jesus was also ready to obey what His Father wanted, no matter how hard it was. In John 5:30, He said that He didn't want to do His will, but only the Father's will. The Prince of Peace knew He would need the Father's help for everything. He said He could do nothing by Himself (see John 5:19b). He would also need a heart that only wanted to please God. In John 8:29, Jesus said He always did the things that pleased His Father. Jesus had the right heart to bring God's Kingdom to earth.

A MIRROR

Have you ever played the "mirror game" when everyone has to copy the leader? Whatever the leader said or did, everyone else has to do the same thing to win.

This is what kind of follower Jesus was when He was here on earth. God's Son was so close to His Father and loved His Father so much that He knew God's voice and what He looked like. His "faith eyes" saw what was happening in Heaven. Jesus was just like a God mirror. That is why Jesus could say, "...*He who has seen Me, has seen the Father...*" (John 14:9).

Jesus had a heart that wanted to obey, and it allowed Him to be filled with the Holy Spirit. That gave Him the power to do the Father's business and destroy the works of the devil. Acts 10:38 says, "*how God anointed Jesus with the Holy Spirit and with power, and how he went about doing good and healing all who were oppressed by the devil, for God was with Him.*"

Right now, Jesus still points to your Heavenly Father. By the same Holy Spirit, you get to discover and show others the Father's heart. Now you get to do the works of the Father, and destroy the works of the devil.

THE FATHER'S HEART

Did you know that the religious leaders during Jesus' time spent their whole lives serving God, but they never knew the Father's heart? How sad! They even became angry at Jesus when He showed them what the Father wanted to do. The leaders thought God only cared about people obeying all the laws and rules. They thought miracles only happened a long time ago. When Jesus did powerful miracles and helped people, He was showing everyone the Father's business.

The leaders did not want to change the way they thought. They did not want to repent. Instead, they called Jesus a liar, and had Him put to death. They did not understand the Father's heart, or feel God's presence. They were not hungry.

AN INVITATION

God's plan for your life is for you to complete your royal mission. But it is more than just doing powerful things like miracles. The real reason for miracles and healing people is to show the huge, great, wonderful and loving heart that the Father has for people. Every miracle is an invitation to see the Father Himself. The Father's heart and love is the most important thing in the whole world. Everything about Jesus and the gospel is a story about the

Father's love. He is calling the hearts of all people to come to Him.

THE REST OF THE STORY

People can go all over the world and tell others about Jesus, and that is good. People will get saved. But if the Father's heart is not shown, it is like telling only part of the story, and leaving out the exciting ending. When Jesus was 12 years old, He told us something really important: to be about our Father's business. The Father's business comes from the heart of God. When you discover this, you will:

GET TO SHOW GOD'S POWER LIKE JESUS DID.

HAVE JOY.

FEEL GOD'S PRESENCE.

Bringing God's Kingdom to earth will be fun! It's for everyone!

A TARGET FOR LOVE

Even though you may be young, you get to bring God's presence and show the Father's heart wherever you go. It could be at your school, church, at home, or even at the store. Everyone, no matter where they might be, can be a target for God's love.

One of our young leaders, a 12-year-old girl named Serena, was in a store one day and saw a little girl. As she looked at her, Serena saw with her "faith eyes," a picture of Jesus holding the little girl in His arms. Serena told her mom what she had just seen and asked, "Should I go tell her?" Serena was a bit shy and did not go over and talk to the little girl or her mother. But she kept seeing them while they were in the store. Finally, in the parking lot, Serena got brave and told the girl's mom, "I just saw your daughter in the arms of Jesus."

The mom began to cry and said, "You don't know what that means to me. I have been so afraid. I've been having nightmares about bad things happening to my child, and now I feel she will be okay and that she is safe. Thank you so much!"

When you give away what God has given you, God's Kingdom of light comes to where the kingdom of darkness once ruled. As a child of the King, it is one of the most special things you can do.

ROYAL RICHES

So far, you have been discovering wonderful and amazing things about who you are and what you have been given by your heavenly Papa.

You are a:

ROYAL PRINCE OR PRINCESS.

PRECIOUS CHILD OF THE KING.

COSTLY TREASURE.

For your royal mission you have:

- The keys of power and authority.

- The Holy Spirit—who is your friend, leader, and guide.

- The presence of God Himself.

- His anointing, which is the power of God, smeared all over you.

- Faith that can see invisible worlds.

- Prayer that can bring Heaven to earth.

- The Father's heart that brings joy, power, and love to those who are hungry and hurting.

Don't you feel rich? You are! Don't you feel special? You are!

EVEN MORE TREASURE

As you follow God, your royal mission will become more exciting, with more adventures waiting for you. Here are some things that will help you discover even more treasure in the Kingdom:

THE WORKS OF THE FATHER

Prayer—Ask God to use you to show His Kingdom to others. Ask for miracles to happen wherever you go.

God's Word—Invite the Holy Spirit to show you things when you read God's Word. Read about Jesus, and how He showed people the Kingdom of God and the Father's heart.

Read—Read books about God's heroes, and those who brought God's Kingdom to earth.

Receive Prayer—Ask people who are anointed, (those who show God's power) to pray for you. You will get what they have!

Hang Out With Heroes—You know all about how David killed Goliath. But did you know that at least four other giants were killed by men who followed David, the first giant killer? Spend time with people who have a heart like yours. Be around those people who are doing great things with God.

Jesus said, "...*As the Father has sent me, I also send you*" (John 20:21). He did the works of the Father, and now you can do them too!

In the next chapter, you will be given even more to complete your royal mission!

TIME WITH YOUR KING

The only way Jesus could do the Father's business was by being very close to Him.

Jesus spent time listening to His Father.

He prayed and talked to Him.

He was able to see the Father with His faith eyes.

He could hear His Father's voice.

In a quiet place, enter into the Father's presence.

Thank Him for His goodness.

Tell Him how much you love Him.

Listen to what He says.

Let Him show you His works.

Let Him show you His heart.

Tell Him you will do whatever He shows you.

Let Him know how much you need Him.

Tell Him how much you want to please your Papa.

JOURNAL TIME

Write down what the Father showed you about His works.

_____

_____

_____

_____

_____

Write about or draw what the Father's heart looks like.

_____

_____

_____

_____

JOURNEY ADVENTURES

Ask the Holy Spirit to take you on a Kingdom Adventure.

Let the Father show you someone you can pray for.

See what the Father is doing.

Do what the Father is doing.

Do what He shows you.

Write what happened.

_____

_____

_____

_____

_____

_____

CHAPTER 10

NICE IS NOT ENOUGH

Having good character is really important. What is character? It is how you act and behave. It tells everyone what kind of person you are.

If you have good character, you are:

- Honest—you don't lie or cheat.

- Kind—you help people, and you are not mean.

- Polite—you respect others.

- Trustworthy—people trust you and believe what you say.

- Humble—you don't brag or put others down.

- A sharing person—you give what you have to others.

Many people believe that having good character is the most important thing a Christian can have. You should have good character. Jesus was polite, honest, kind, and humble. Some people think that good character is even more important than having God's power. You should be nice. But, *nice is not enough!* The devil is not afraid of nice. He will just leave you alone if that is all you have. Being nice and having good character cannot do anything to defeat the kingdom of darkness.

YOUR ROYAL MISSION

Do you remember what your royal mission is?

You are here to:

SHOW OTHERS THE FATHER'S HEART AND LOVE.

DO HIS GOOD WORKS— INCLUDING MIRACLES!

DESTROY THE WORKS OF THE DEVIL.

BRING HEAVEN TO EARTH.

Your royal mission is to change the world! What did Jesus need to do the works of the Father? God's power.

YOU CAN HAVE BOTH!

Having just good character and being nice will not show people what God's Kingdom looks like. You need God's power *and* good character. Jesus had both. So...how can you have good character and God's power like Jesus? *Obey* God.

Jesus told His followers to go and teach people how to live. He told them to heal the sick, raise the dead, and set people free from the devil. (See Matthew 10:8.) That is what a follower of Jesus does. When you obey what Jesus says to do, miracles will happen. That is when you start to look and act like Jesus.

Some people think they need more character before they can do miracles. Jesus never said you need more character to show His power.

HOW DO YOU ACT?

You are a royal prince or princess. Your Father is the Creator of the universe. Your big brother, Jesus, is the King of all kings. Someone who rules over a kingdom, like you, acts and behaves in a special way.

As a royal child, you:

HAVE COURAGE.

LOVE YOUR HEAVENLY FATHER VERY MUCH.

USE YOUR POWER AND AUTHORITY
TO HONOR GOD.

SHOW OTHERS WHAT HEAVEN IS LIKE.

SHOW GOOD CHARACTER.

POWER TO GROW

For you to be like Jesus, you need the power of the Holy Spirit. Remember what happened to people when they were preparing to be a king or prophet? They were anointed, or smeared with oil, so they could do special things. It is the anointing of the Holy Spirit that makes you look, think, and act like Jesus.

You may see someone at school who tells you he feels sick. You feel that God wants you to pray for that person. When you obey and say "yes," the Holy Spirit will do two things. First, He will "leak" on the *outside* of you and do a miracle. Second, He will help you on the *inside* to become more like Jesus.

THE PURPOSE OF POWER

Some people think that the only reason we have God's power is so we won't sin anymore. That may sound good, but it's not right. The power of sin was already broken when Jesus died on the Cross. Jesus won the battle, and now we have the prize He won for us. We have the keys of power and authority.

The Bible says that you are a new person because Jesus is in your heart (see 2 Corinthians 5:17). Sin no longer has any power over you. That means you don't have to sin anymore! You don't need power to fight something that is already dead.

You have God's power so you so you can show everyone what Heaven is like. God's Kingdom is a world full of miracles. God's presence and power makes miracles happen. Do you know another reason you need power? Boldness! God's power in you means you can have courage to do impossible things. Being bold means that you are not afraid to obey God. You do not need to be afraid of the devil or what he does to people.

DANGEROUS!

Your heavenly Papa really wants you to be *dangerous*—not just nice! Who do you think was the most dangerous person on earth? *Jesus!* He is very dangerous to the devil and his kingdom of darkness. Jesus came to earth to destroy the works of the devil. All of the demons are still afraid of Him today. They even fear His name. As soon as Jesus gave you the keys of power and authority, *you* became dangerous, too!

Your good character is important to your Father. But do you know what? You cannot make yourself good. It only happens when you want to obey God and do what He wants you to do. Jesus said, "*I do not seek my own will, but the will of Him who sent Me*" (see John 5:30). It is easy to obey God when you love Him.

POWER CLOTHES

Jesus wanted His followers to show everyone what His Kingdom was like, but they would need power to do it. Before Jesus went back to Heaven, He told them to wait for the Holy Spirit to come. (See Acts 1:4,5.) For days and days His followers waited in a room. Then, the Holy Spirit came...with *power*. It changed them, *and* it changed the world! The Bible says they were clothed with power from Heaven. That day the Holy Spirit put new power clothes on the followers of Jesus.

That is how character and power comes. It happens when you are in God's presence. It is like being outside in the sunshine. The sun will change the color of your skin. The presence of God will change you too. You will look and act more and more like Him.

A Friend of God

If you were friends with someone, you would not want to make them feel bad, would you? Of course not! The Holy Spirit is the best friend you will ever have. The Bible says that we should not *grieve* Him, or in other words make the Holy Spirit *feel bad* (see Eph. 4:30). Do you know what makes Him feel bad? When we sin. Sin happens when we do wrong things. Sin also happens when we don't do the right things.

Go With the Flow

The Bible also says, "Do not quench the [Holy] Spirit" (1 Thess. 5:19). To *quench* means to "stop the flow." Remember how the Holy Spirit loves to "leak" out of you? He is ready to bring people to you so they can be saved, healed, and set free from the devil. He wants you to follow Him and let His power flow. Showing His power is the best way you can be friends with the Holy Spirit.

Plugged In

Your Father wants you to walk in His power every day. How do you do that? By wanting more and more of Him. The Bible tells us to live in Jesus like you would live in a house. You can have God's life and power when you are that close. It's like being "plugged into" a great power source.

God wants you to be hungry for His power and presence. What does hunger look like? Let's say you know someone who is doing powerful things with God. You want the anointing that they have. You ask that person to pray for you. Your Father will give it to you. One of the best prayers you can ever say is, "More Lord, I want more of You."

GIVE AND GET

What should you do when God gives you His power? Give it away! You can only keep what you give away. God's Kingdom is like that. Do you want to see people get healed? Look for those who are sick. Ask if you can pray for them. You are not the healer, but you are like a server. You can serve and give away what God and Heaven has given you.

Jesus came to earth to show the Father's heart and love for people. It is a story that only someone with the power of the Holy Spirit can show and tell. You can never have too much of His power or character. Remember who you are, and what you get to do.

God does not want you to have just a nice, quiet life. Nice is not enough!

Be *dangerous*!

LOOK, LISTEN, OBEY

So far it has been an exciting adventure finding out who you are, what you have been given, and what you get to do. Three easy ways to help you bring God's Kingdom to earth is:

Look—use your "faith eyes" to see what your Heavenly Father is doing.

Listen—with the "ears" of your heart to what God is saying.

Obey—what the Holy Spirit wants you to do.

There's still more that your Father has for you. He just loves getting you ready for your royal mission!

TIME WITH YOUR KING

Ask your Heavenly Papa to come.

Let the Holy Spirit bring you into His presence.

Tell Papa how great He is.

Tell Him how much you love Him.

Let the Father love on you for awhile.

Ask Him to show you again who you are.

You will see what He sees; a Royal Child.

Take a good look.

In His presence, ask Jesus to give you what He has.

Tell Him you want to be just like Him.

Thank Him for His power.

Thank Him that you don't have to sin anymore.

Thank Him for His courage.

Thank Him for His love.

Let Papa know you want to obey Him.

Let Him know you are hungry.

Be ready to receive His power and character.

JOURNAL TIME

Write or draw what the Father showed you.

_____

_____

_____

_____

_____

What did He see when He looked at you?

_____

_____

_____

_____

_____

_____

_____

What does a royal child look like?

_____

_____

_____

_____

_____

_____

_____

_____

What did Jesus do when you told Him you want to be just like Him?

_____

_____

_____

_____

_____

What did you get from the Father when you said you want to obey Him?

_____

_____

_____

_____

What does His power and character look like?

_____

_____

_____

_____

JOURNEY ADVENTURES

God wants His children to be nice and dangerous. Good character comes when you are hungry for Him. It comes when you want to obey.

Look for someone who is sick or needs prayer.

Ask if you can pray for them.

Let the Holy Spirit help you.

Let Him "leak" out of you.

Write what happened.

_____

_____

_____

_____

_____

Is there someone you know who is doing powerful things with God?

Ask them if they would pray for you.

Thank them.

Write what you received.

_____

_____

_____

_____

_____

_____

_____

_____

_____

_____

_____

CHAPTER 11

FOLLOW THE SIGNS

A God Story

It was a Sunday morning. We were in a church in a small African village. As the service was ending, about 25 women and children came to the front for prayer. Our team began to pray. One by one, each person was healed of sickness and pain. We all saw God's presence and power that morning!

Later that day, a young boy came to our hut. He asked if we would come and pray for his father to be healed. We went to his home and prayed for his father. Right away God's power touched him, and he felt a little better. The next day the boy's father came by and asked if we would pray some more. As we prayed, God healed him!

We could see with our "faith eyes" that something was happening to the man's heart, too. We asked if he would like Jesus to come into his heart, and he said yes. He became a Christian that day. We were so excited about what God had done!

This man had been the leader of the young men in the village. He and the others did not like Christians. When Christian doctors would come to his village, they would cut down thorn bushes and put them on the road so it was hard for people to get through. He would not let Christians come near him.

But when Jesus came into his heart, this man became a new person! He was now our friend. He loved Christians, and he loved God. Everywhere we went, he followed. He even gave us his best goat!

What happened? What made this man so hungry for prayer? His son, who was very sick, was healed that Sunday morning. When the father saw his son healed, it made him hungry. When God healed the father's sickness, it was a sign of His power and love. That made the father want something better, even greater than being healed. He wanted God Himself! That is what made him say "yes" when we asked him if he wanted Jesus to come into his heart.

REVIVAL!

Revival! You may never have heard this word before, but it is a special word. Revival happens when God's power is shown. It happens when Heaven comes to earth, and people see God's Kingdom. When revival comes, things change. People repent, and change the way they think. People who love God can make changes in schools, churches, stores, playgrounds, and homes. Whole cities and even countries can change. People turn to God, and their faith eyes open. Peace, healing, and joy come. The kingdom of darkness gets smaller. Anger, sickness, and fear go away. God's Kingdom of light rules.

SIGNS, SIGNS, SIGNS

"Signs and wonders" help bring revival because people see miracles. They see God's presence and power.

Signs are everywhere. They are very important. They tell you where you are. They tell you where you are going. Without them you might get lost.

Have you ever gone on a trip to a fun and exciting place? Where did you go? Was it on a camping trip, a vacation to Disneyland, or a safari in Africa? Maybe there was a sign along the way that said you were almost there. You probably got excited when you saw it, right? But you didn't want to stop and stay at the sign, did you? Of course not! Why? Because the sign was pointing to something even better. It made you want to hurry and get to that fun and exciting place.

God's signs, wonders, and miracles are just like that. They help bring revival—they point the way to something even greater. Let's find out what God's signs show us. Let's see where they take us if we follow them.

SIGNS AND WONDERS
SHOW WHAT GOD IS LIKE

You are here to be a witness for God. A witness is someone who tells and shows others what they have seen or know. To be a witness for God means to show God's power. That means miracles, signs, and wonders, and they happen when you pray for people. Without signs and wonders, people won't get to see who God really is. They will miss seeing His powerful love, and how much He really cares for people.

SIGNS AND WONDERS
HELP PEOPLE CHOOSE RIGHT OR WRONG

In Luke chapter 5, there is an exciting story about a great miracle. Peter was fishing all night long, but didn't catch anything. Jesus told him to throw out his net one more time on the other side of the boat. Even though there were no fish around, Peter obeyed. Surprise! So many fish were caught in the net that the boat almost sank.

Peter saw this as a sign of God's power and said, "Jesus, I am a man full of sin" (see Luke 5:8). Jesus didn't tell Peter he was a sinner, did He? Miracles are like when a light is turned on. The light can show what is in our hearts. It can also show us if there is sin in our lives. Signs and wonders can help us be sorry for our sins, and repent.

Sometimes people choose not to follow God when they see miracles. Pharaoh, the king of Egypt, turned against the Hebrews when he saw the signs and wonders of the ten plagues. The Bible says his heart was hard. (See Exodus 9:35.) The religious leaders also turned against Jesus even after they saw all of His great miracles. They would not repent either. When people see signs and wonders they will choose to come to God's love, or they will turn away from Him.

SIGNS AND WONDERS GIVE US COURAGE

It is so important to tell others about the miracles God has done and is doing. Stories about signs and wonders are called "testimonies." It is important to hear testimonies, too. Why? Because "God Stories" will remind

you how great and wonderful your heavenly Father is. They will also remind you how special you are as a son or daughter of the King. When you hear about God's power and how it destroys the works of the devil, you get courage—you'll be brave. And you won't be afraid of the enemy.

There was once a group of brave warriors. They were called the sons of Ephraim. They could shoot arrows better than any army. But on the day the battle started, they were afraid, and ran away! Why? What happened? The Bible says they turned away from God. (See Psalms 78:10.) They stopped obeying Him. They had forgotten about all the signs and wonders, and miracles God had shown them. When the sons of Ephraim forgot how powerful their heavenly Father was, they forgot who they were. They lost their courage to fight and win the battle.

MIRACLES SHOW GOD'S GLORY

In John chapter 2 there is a story about how Jesus went to a wedding. Soon, all the wine was gone. Jesus had not done any miracles yet, but Mary, His mom, knew who her son was. Mary told Jesus, "We have no wine." Jesus said, "It is not the time yet for me to do miracles and be glorified." Mary told the servers, "Do whatever He tells you."

Remember how Jesus only did what He saw His Father do? He didn't see His Father turning water into wine at first. When Mary used her faith and told everyone to do what her son said, something happened in Heaven. Jesus looked at His Father again. He saw His Father turning water into wine.

Mary's faith changed Heaven! Now was the time for Jesus to be glorified. Jesus' first miracle happened because of His mom's faith. Her faith moved Heaven. This sign and wonder, this miracle, glorified Jesus. When miracles happen, God is glorified. His power and greatness pushes away satan's kingdom of darkness. Light always chases away darkness. Just turn on a light in a dark room. What happens? The room is not dark—darkness turned to light.

God's presence and power is the light. The glory of God is the light that makes darkness disappear. What happens when the kingdom of darkness leaves? God's Kingdom of light takes its place. The Kingdom of Heaven now rules. God is glorified!

You get to bring God's Kingdom of light and glory to a place where there used to be only darkness.

SIGNS HELP PEOPLE GIVE GLORY TO GOD

In the Bible, Matthew 9:8 says that when the people saw the man healed, they glorified God. This story is about a man who could not move. Jesus met him, and forgave his sins. Then He told the man to get up and walk. When the man got up and walked, all the people started to praise God and give Him glory. They shouted out how great God is.

When signs, wonders, and miracles happen, people react. When people see God's power destroy the works of the devil, something happens inside of them. Their hearts open up like a gate, and you know what comes out? *Praise!* It's just like how you feel when your favorite team wins, only better! The more you hear about testimonies and "God Stories," the more your heart will praise and glorify your Father. Yeah God!

SIGNS AND WONDERS TELL US WHO JESUS IS

Jesus told the Jews that He was their Savior. Many did not believe Him. Then He said, "*though you do not believe Me, believe the works, so that you may know and understand that the Father is in Me, and I in the Father*" (John 10:38). Jesus knew if people would follow the signs of His miracles, then many would come to Him and believe. Miracles tell us who Jesus really is.

MIRACLES HELP PEOPLE HEAR GOD'S VOICE

When people hear testimonies of God's power, it turns their hearts toward Heaven. It reminds them that God's invisible Kingdom is more real than what they see with their eyeballs. People repent and change the way they think. Miracles help people repent. Miracles also make people hungry for God. When they hear the good news about a good God, they want some too. The ears of their hearts open, and they will hear what the Father has to say to them.

MIRACLES TELL US ABOUT JESUS AND HIS CHURCH

The Bible says Jesus is the head, or leader, of the church. (See Ephesians 5:23.) We are His followers. We are called His Body, or the Church. (See 1 Corinthians 12:27.) The head would never leave the body, would it? That would be silly! Jesus made a promise to you. He said He would never leave you.

God's presence comforts us, brings us close to Him, and makes us feel special. His presence also gives us courage to show His great power and love. When miracles happen, it proves that God Himself is with you. It is how you can complete your royal mission, and bring Heaven to earth.

Signs and wonders are very important. They point the way to something that is greater. They point to God, Himself! Signs help us to go to new places. Your Heavenly Father and His Holy Spirit want to take you to new places. He has new and exciting adventures in His Kingdom for you to see, hear, and enjoy. His presence and power will lead you—just follow the signs.

TIME WITH YOUR KING

Invite God's presence.

Thank Him for who He is.

Thank Him for His kindness, care, and His power.

Thank Him for being such a loving Papa.

Ask the Father what revival looks like.

Let Him show you what He sees when He looks at your:

SCHOOL

PLAYGROUND

CHURCH

HOME

Ask Him for His Kingdom to come to those places.

Ask Him for signs and wonders.

Ask Him for revival.

Let Him show you His glory.

Ask Him to use you.

JOURNAL TIME

Write down and draw a picture of what revival would look like where you live.

_____

_____

_____

_____

_____

What does God's glory look like?

_____

_____

_____

_____

_____

_____

Search through your Bible and find at least three signs, wonders, or miracles.

_____

_____

_____

_____

_____

_____

_____

JOURNEY ADVENTURES

Begin to pray for revival, for signs and wonders in your:

School

_____

Playground

_____

Church

_____

Home

_____

Start looking with your "faith eyes" when you go to these places. Pray what you "see."

Share testimonies or "God Stories" with your family at home.

Share with your friends at your school, church, and playground.

Write what happens.

_____

_____

_____

_____

_____

_____

_____

_____

_____

_____

_____

_____

CHAPTER 12

TREASURE FOR EVERYONE

God made a promise when He said, "I will be with you" (Matt. 28:20). He said it because of His great love, and He loves being with you! God's presence is not only a love gift, but it is also where courage comes from.

Why do you need courage? So you can complete your royal mission. When Heaven comes to earth, the works of the devil are broken. The kingdom of darkness is pushed away, and satan loses. It takes courage to be an ambassador, and bring Heaven to earth. It takes courage to change the world!

God's presence in you makes your heart a treasure chest. Heroes in the Bible had this treasure, and changed the world:

APOSTLE PAUL PREACHED THE GOSPEL
TO MANY PEOPLE.

KING DAVID RULED A NATION.

MOSES LED THE HEBREWS OUT OF EGYPT AND SLAVERY.

GIDEON LED THE ISRAELITES INTO VICTORY AGAINST GREAT ENEMIES.

Jesus told His followers to go into the world to preach the gospel and do miracles. They would show the people what the Kingdom of God looks like. His followers were not perfect people. But Jesus asked them to change the world, and they did! It happened because Jesus said, "I will be with you." He will be with you too!

CARRYING HIS PRESENCE

Everyone who is a Christian has God's promise of "I will be with you." So, how do you carry God's presence with you?

It happens when you:

- Know that you have a great treasure inside of you.

- Spend time loving Papa each day.

- Talk, act, and have attitudes that please the Holy Spirit.

- Are careful to not make the Holy Spirit feel bad.

- Want to put God first in everything.

Walking with God this way let's the Holy Spirit do powerful things. Each day becomes an exciting adventure.

DON'T HIDE THE TREASURE

God's presence in you can be seen because of the anointing. Remember what the "anointing" means? *Smeared* and covered with God's power-filled presence. Miracles happen when you walk covered by and "leaking" the Holy Spirit. God does not want you to keep and enjoy His anointing just for yourself. Don't hide the treasure that is in you! Remember, in the Kingdom of God you only get to keep what you give away.

A GOOD KING

There was once a very rich king who ruled a great land. The people were happy and loved the king because he was a good ruler. One day a terrible storm came and destroyed all the crops. Soon, everyone would be hungry. What do you think the good king did? He used his riches to buy food for the people he loved. They would not go hungry.

You are like that rich king. You are a royal ruler, too. Your treasure chest filled with God's presence is to be given to people who are hungry for the Father. Because you have been given so much from your heavenly Papa, you have so much to share with others. God wants you to give others a chance to see, hear, and feel His presence. Meeting God is what changes people's lives.

Having God's anointing on you makes it possible for others to meet God. It will happen through you. If peanut butter was smeared all over you, what would happen if you started touching your friends? What would happen if your parents hugged you? The peanut butter would rub off on everyone.

In the same way, when you are smeared with God's presence, the Holy Spirit "rubs off" on everyone you touch. When He rubs off on others, guess what happens? People get healed, fear and anger leave, people are not bothered by the devil anymore. The anointing breaks the chains that satan puts on people.

God "rubs off" a lot when you share His Word and pray for people. But there are other ways, too. It can happen all the time!

A BIG ROCK

Good things can happen, and lives can change just because you and God "show up" together. It's like carrying a big rock. What happens when you drop a rock in a puddle of water? There is a big splash, and waves push the water away. When you go to school, to the store, or anywhere, you can make a big splash, too. You and God's presence can push away the kingdom of darkness.

Jesus said you can even leave His peace wherever you go. Sometimes people will feel different because you gave away God's presence in a place. The devil and his unseen world, the kingdom of darkness, are afraid of you because of what you carry—God's presence.

JESUS GOES FOR A WALK

One day Jesus was walking down a road. It wasn't long until there was a crowd of people around Jesus. They all wanted to be close to Him. A sick woman reached out and touched His robe. Suddenly, Jesus stopped and asked, "Who touched My garments?" (Mark 5:30). His disciples were surprised when Jesus asked that question. They thought, "Everyone touched you, Jesus. This is a big crowd!" But Jesus said He felt power flow out of Him. The anointing of the Holy Spirit that was on Jesus rubbed off onto the sick woman. Her faith made the Holy Spirit "leak" out of Him. The chains of sickness that the devil put on the woman were broken. She was now healed and free!

You have the same anointing and power that Jesus has. The Holy Spirit will tell you when you can pour out God's presence. Miracles happen when you let the Holy Spirit do what He wants to do. Just let God smear you with Himself!

A FULL BUCKET

You owe people a chance to meet God. Your Father wants everybody to have what you have, His presence. Being full of God's Holy Spirit is the only way it can happen. Only a full bucket can be poured out. Papa God just loves to pour out His Spirit on you. It pleases Him to see you overflow and "leak." He never runs out of promises. So get filled over and over again!

AMAZING ANGELS

Angels are amazing creatures. They are powerful and full of glory. Angels spend a lot of time in Heaven worshiping God. Whenever angels came to earth, the Bible says people would bow down and worship them. We should not worship angels, but we need to know what their job is. Angels are sent to earth to help us when we show others God's Kingdom. They are needed when Heaven comes to earth.

Most angels are bored! Why? Because they are waiting to help people like you who want to do impossible things, like miracles. Angels get excited and love to be around boys and girls who are nice *and* dangerous. Being "dangerous" keeps angels really busy! They will always follow those who walk by faith with the Holy Spirit, and use their "faith eyes."

Angels are awesome. They will protect you and help others receive from God. These helpers from Heaven want to be on your winning team.

SENT FROM HEAVEN

As you go on your journey to complete your royal mission, remember that angels are ready to help you do amazing and exciting things. How do they come to help? The Bible says that angels are sent when people pray. They come to help answer your prayers.

You are from another world. You are a royal child of the King. Wherever you go, you bring an "Open Heaven" with you. What does that mean? You are like a gate or ladder to Heaven. Angels will come, and God will send from Heaven what is needed to show His love and power to people. Heaven will follow you.

Angels also listen for God's voice and word. They will go and do whatever the Father says. When you speak and echo what the Father's heart says, guess what happens? Angels hear what you say. It sounds just like Papa God. They come down from Heaven to make sure that what you prayed about will happen. That is why you can pray with boldness. You don't have to be shy. You have the keys of power and authority. The angels are listening! They are excited about helping you give away your treasure!

SURPRISES! A GOD STORY

One Sunday morning, I was teaching in Children's Church. Suddenly, there was an "explosion" of colored feathers in the air! A second later, *poof*, more feathers appeared out of nowhere. As the green, yellow, red, and purple feathers floated to the floor, the children jumped up and climbed over the chairs to catch them. There was laughter and shouts of joy at this sign and wonder!

There are many ways God lets us know when He "shows up" in a place. Sometimes people will fall on the floor. Sometimes they will start laughing. (God likes to tickle His kids.) I have seen oil and gold dust cover the hands of children and grownups. We have even smelled and tasted God's presence in our classroom!

Your Father likes surprises. He is not hiding in a plain, boring box. He likes to do different things, just so you can wonder about Him. With every sign or surprise, we discover how amazing our Papa is. He has a lot more surprises to show you! Keep following the signs! You will discover that there is treasure for everyone!

In the next chapter, you are going to make another amazing discovery. You'll find out what it means to be like Jesus.

TIME WITH YOUR KING

Ask the Holy Spirit to take you into the presence of the Father.

Thank your Papa for His promise to be with you.

Thank Him for His love gift.

Tell Him how much you like to be with Him.

Thank your Father for the treasure that is in your heart.

Thank Him that you get to carry His presence.

Let the Holy Spirit "smear" you with Himself.

Tell Him you want to give your great treasure away to hungry people.

Ask the Father to show you His angels.

JOURNAL TIME

Write down and draw what the treasure in your heart looks like.

_____

_____

_____

_____

_____

What is it like to be "smeared" with God, the Holy Spirit?

_____

_____

_____

_____

_____

_____

_____

_____

_____

_____

_____

_____

_____

_____

Draw a picture and write about the angels that God showed you.

_____

_____

_____

_____

_____

_____

_____

JOURNEY ADVENTURES

Ask the Holy Spirit to lead you to a place where He could "rub off" on someone.

Wherever you go, pray for God's peace and Kingdom to come.

Look for someone you can give your treasure to.

Let the Holy Spirit "leak out" at your school, where you play, and at your home.

Write about all the things that happened.

_____

_____

_____

_____

_____

_____

CHAPTER 13

JUST LIKE JESUS

Jesus! When you hear or see that name, what pictures do you see in your mind? What words do you think of?

One day the apostle John saw Jesus in a vision (that's a picture you see with your "faith eyes"). John saw Jesus with hair like wool that was white as snow. His eyes were like flames of fire. His feet looked like shiny metal. When John heard Jesus' voice, it sounded like a loud waterfall. (See Revelation 1:13-16.)

Jesus is in Heaven. He sits on a throne right next to the Father. His glory is as bright as the sun. Angels and other creatures worship Him without stopping. Jesus has won the victory, and all His enemies are now at His feet.

It is really, really important for you to see Jesus. It is important for you to know what He is like today. Why?

Because in First John 4:17, it says something amazing: *"As He* [Jesus] *is, so also are we in this world!"*

The Bible says you are just like Jesus is today. How can that be true? That sounds impossible! Well, it *is* impossible by yourself. But remember your best friend, the Holy Spirit? God, the Holy Spirit, does many things for you because you are so special and loved by God. He comforts you, He gives you gifts, and He covers you with His power. He does all those things so you can be like Jesus.

A PERFECT MODEL

Have you ever seen an artist take a piece of clay and make a statue out of it? Sometimes the artist looks at a model. He tries to make the clay statue look just like the model. That is what the Holy Spirit does. He is like the artist. You are like the clay. Jesus is the model.

When Jesus went back to Heaven, He became the perfect model. He is full of glory, full of power, full of victory. Now the artist, the Holy Spirit, comes and makes us look like Jesus.

THE CROSS

What Jesus did on the Cross is really special and important. The Cross reminds us how much God loves

us. It tells us that the wonderful blood of Jesus washed away all the power of sin in our lives forever. The Cross means we can be one of God's royal children. But the Cross is just the beginning of what it means to be a Christian.

Jesus is not on the Cross anymore! He arose from the dead. He is alive! That is how Jesus is today. Jesus' power over sin and death is what gives you power to be a royal ruler!

Some people are still sad and feel bad that Jesus died on the Cross. Jesus doesn't want you to feel sad, He wants you to thank Him for what He did! When Jesus was beaten and died on the Cross:

HE BECAME POOR, SO YOU COULD BE RICH.

HE WAS WHIPPED AND HURT,
SO YOU COULD BE HEALED AND WELL.

HE TOOK OUR SIN, SO YOU COULD BE
FORGIVEN AND FREE FROM SIN.

Jesus became like the people in the world—poor, sick, and full of sin—so we could be like Him! We can be like He is *now*.

You could never pay back to the Father what His Son did for you. The best thing you can do to honor and thank Jesus is to be just like Him.

LOOK UP, NOT IN

Remember when Jesus said, "*I can do nothing*" (John 5:19)? He knew He was just a man. He couldn't do any miracles by Himself. Did that make Jesus feel sad? Did He walk around feeling sorry for Himself? Did He look in the mirror and think He was a weak person? No way! What did He do? Jesus just looked up at His Father in Heaven. He followed the Holy Spirit. He let God "leak" out of Him.

Some people forget what Jesus did for them. They might look at themselves and see how weak they are. They may even talk about how bad they were. They may think about their old sins, even after the Father has forgiven them! These are just tricks and lies of the devil. Your Father doesn't want you to look down on yourself. Royal rulers don't look at themselves, they look up to their King. Jesus depended on His Father and changed the world. You can too!

The Holy Spirit made you like Jesus. You are a special treasure. Because your Papa is so rich and powerful, you don't have to talk about being weak. Don't agree with satan's lies. If the devil says you can't do anything right, or you are dumb, or weak, don't agree with him. Only agree with God and say, "*I am strong! I can do all things in Jesus!*" (see Phil. 4:13).

Say those things loud enough so you can hear it with your ears. It is good when you can hear yourself agree with God. Use you "faith eyes" and mouth. See what your Father sees in you, and then agree. When you do that, you get blessed. You get good things from the Father. You feel close to Him. It also blesses God, too. When you say who you are, you are saying God did a great job in making you, loving you, and saving you! Your Father is never praised or lifted up when you put yourself down.

BEING LIKE HIM

The Bible says that as Jesus was so are we in this world (see 1 John 4:17). Jesus is sitting on a throne in Heaven. He is awesome and wonderful. He is full of glory. He is full of power. He has won the victory, and He is holy. This is who Jesus is. He wants you to have all that He has. Here are four special things that Jesus wants to give you. He wants you to show these things to others so they can see His Kingdom on earth.

Glory: Jesus lives inside everyone who has been saved and forgiven of sin. But the glory of God seems to be on just a few people. When the glory and presence of Jesus is on someone, it is almost like bright sunshine, or a fire that is burning. When Jesus' disciples were filled with the baptism of the Holy Spirit, there were flames of fire over each person's head. No one could explain it, but it was the glory of God that came into that room.

Even today people might see fire when God's presence is very strong on people. Satan and his kingdom of darkness cannot put this fire out. It is much greater than anything he has. Jesus said He is coming back for a Church (full of royal rulers) that is full of His glory. Ask Him for His glory to come on you.

Power: As Jesus sits on His throne, power flows from Him. If you are like Him then you will show His power, too. The Baptism of the Holy Spirit puts "power clothes" on you. When you put on a new coat or hat, everyone will see it, won't they? In the same way, people will also see your "power clothes." They will see your power when they see miracles and feel God's presence on you.

The Bible says that it is the power of God that:

SAVES PEOPLE.

HEALS SICK AND HURTING BODIES.

TAKES AWAY FEAR AND BAD THOUGHTS
FROM PEOPLE'S MINDS.

FORGIVES AND MAKES YOU
BECOME A CHILD OF GOD.

MAKES OUR SPIRITS LIVE FOREVER
WITH PAPA GOD.

Showing the power of Jesus shows the world the Kingdom of Heaven.

Victory: Jesus beat all of His enemies. He beat the powers of darkness and hell. He beat death, sin, and the works of the devil. Jesus was raised from the dead and sits next to His Father. His glory is all around Him. Everything that has a name, every power is at His feet. He won the victory, He has the keys, and so do you!

Have you ever seen a champion team or someone who won a great contest? How did the winners act? Were they happy? Did they show everyone their trophy? They may have lost some games in the past, but they don't act like losers when they win, do they? They act like winners. This is how God wants you to act—like a winner. The Bible says that you are *more* than a winner in Jesus. (See Romans 8:37.) You are more than a winner because you did not have to fight the devil to win. Jesus gave you His trophy, the keys of power and authority. You were given the prize He won.

The devil will still want to fight. He doesn't want you to complete your royal mission to bring Heaven to earth. You don't have to be afraid of anything in the kingdom of darkness. You will win those battles, because you are a winner.

Holy: Jesus is perfect and holy. Everything that is evil is far away from Him. Everything that is good is all around Him. You are close to Him, too. Being holy is not just how you act and do things. It is not just obeying rules. Being holy is not what you can and cannot do. The Bible talks about the *beauty* of holiness.

Holiness is something that comes out of you because you love Papa God so much. Holiness comes out because you are so thankful for what Jesus did. Holiness comes out when you follow your friend, the Holy Spirit. When you show God's power, people see God's heart. When you show God's holiness, people see God's beauty.

When you know who you are in this world, you will look and walk like Jesus. People will see His Kingdom. People will see Heaven come to earth. God's love, beauty, and power will be shown. Revival will happen! You will complete your royal mission.

TIME WITH YOUR KING

As you come into the presence of your Father, thank Him for what He has given you.

Thank Him for who you are.

Ask the Father to show you His Son, Jesus.

What does He look like?

What is He doing?

What is He saying?

Come closer to King Jesus.

Ask Him for His Glory.

Ask Him for His power.

Receive His power.

He will make you feel like a winner.

He will give you His holiness.

Thank Him and love on Him.

JOURNAL TIME

Write down and draw what Jesus looks like.

_____

_____

_____

_____

_____

What was it like to receive Jesus' glory, power, victory, and holiness?

_____

_____

_____

_____

_____

_____

_____

_____

_____

_____

_____

_____

_____

Draw a picture of yourself. Do you look like Jesus?

JOURNEY ADVENTURES

After spending some time in the presence of your Papa, look for ways you can show others God's Kingdom.

Pray for someone who is sick or hurting.

Walk around your school or playground, and ask for God's Kingdom to come.

Pray for your teachers.

_____

_____

_____

Pray for your friends.

_____

_____

_____

Write what happened.

_____

_____

_____

_____

_____

_____

_____

_____

_____

_____

_____

_____

CHAPTER 14

CLIMBING MOUNTAINS

A GOD STORY

Every week we would take teams of students and go to different schools, and share about God's love and His Kingdom. The young boys and girls learned about their heavenly Father and how special they were to Him. Many children asked Jesus to come into their hearts, and were healed when God touched them. But that was just the beginning.

As God's love and power came to the classrooms and miracles happened, something else came—God's Kingdom. The children started to act differently. School teachers began to notice that the students were obeying them. People felt a peace all around the school as the children were being friendly and kind to each other.

Some of the boys and girls would write about God's love being in their heart when the teachers gave them writing assignments!

When Heaven comes to earth and touches a place like a school, home, or playground, there is a change that takes place. The kingdom of darkness is pushed away. God's healing love and peace comes. Sin, sickness, anger, and fighting leave.

SALT AND LIGHT

Jesus said some very interesting things about you in Matthew 5:13-16. He said you were like salt and light. Why would He say that? Salt and light are two very powerful things. Salt changes the flavor of food. Salt also keeps food from spoiling. Whenever a light is turned on, the darkness leaves. In other words, salt and light will change whatever is around them. That is the way your heavenly Father looks at you, His Church, and His Kingdom. You get to change whatever is around you!

God's thoughts about you are awesome and amazing. His plans for you are exciting and powerful. He sees you as a son or daughter whom He loves. The Father wants you to bring His Kingdom wherever you live, and wherever you go. When that happens, things change. Every time you tell someone about God's love and they ask Jesus into their heart, the kingdom of darkness loses. Every time you pray for someone and a miracle happens, the works of the devil are destroyed. When you ask God to touch a person, a life is changed. Papa God gets so excited when He sees you doing the same things, and even greater things than His Son Jesus did when He was on earth!

He enjoys putting His "lights" in dark places so His glory, love, and power will shine! Isaiah 60:2 says, "*darkness will cover the earth...But the Lord will rise upon you and His glory will appear upon you.*"

THE MOUNTAINS

So where does God want you to go on your royal mission and spread His Kingdom? The mountains. Your life is made up of many different parts, or "mountains." What are some of the parts, or "mountains" in your life?

YOUR SCHOOL.

YOUR CHURCH.

YOUR FAMILY.

WHERE YOU PLAY.

WHAT KINDS OF MOVIES
AND SHOWS YOU SEE.

HOW RICH OR POOR
ARE THE PEOPLE WHO LIVE NEAR YOU.
THE PEACE OR FIGHTING AROUND YOU.
SICK OR HEALTHY PEOPLE.

KING OF THE MOUNTAIN

When I was young my friends and I would sometimes play a game called, "King of the Mountain." One of us would be "king" and go to the top of a hill. The rest of us would charge up the hill and try to push the "king" down to the bottom of the hill. Whoever pushed the "king" down became the new "king."

These areas of life, or mountains, are very important to God and His Kingdom of Heaven. They are also important to the devil and his kingdom of darkness. Whatever kingdom rules on top of these "mountains" or areas of life, rules over the lives of people.

If the kingdom of darkness rules:

- Schools and playgrounds are not safe.

- Families are unhappy.

- Ungodly shows and movies are made.

- People are poor and sick.

- There is no peace, only fighting and wars.

If the Kingdom of Heaven rules on these mountains:

- Schools are safe, Godly things are taught.
- Playgrounds are safe.
- Churches are full of God's presence and power.
- Families are happy and together.
- Godly movies and television shows are made.
- People are not sick or poor.
- There is peace.

GET READY TO CLIMB

Your Father has been getting you ready for your royal mission to bring His Kingdom to earth. He is taking you on a journey that leads to the mountains. You might say, "I have never climbed a mountain, how do I do it?" That's OK. Papa God is about to show you.

A FAMOUS MOUNTAIN CLIMBER

Some of the greatest heroes in the Bible were young men. God would put them in dark places so that His light would shine. They learned how to climb the mountains and change nations!

One of these heroes was a boy named Daniel. (See Daniel 1-4.) He was just a teenager when he was taken

away from his family. When the king heard that Daniel was very smart and full of wisdom, he brought him into his court. Soon Daniel became the king's closest helper because of his wisdom, power, and because he could be trusted.

Right now you might think, "Wow, climbing mountains is easy, Daniel gets to be with the king!" Well, it's not that easy. The country that Daniel lived in was one of the darkest, most sinful places on earth. He was surrounded by evil magicians. The wicked king made everybody worship idols, and he let satan's kingdom rule. Even though Daniel was taken away from his mom and dad and had to live in an ungodly place full of temptation, he was not angry at God. Daniel loved God and would follow Him. Daniel knew his royal mission.

Because he served a great God, Daniel was protected from the evil that surrounded him. His heart was so close to Papa God's goodness, love, and power, that sin could not touch God's holiness in Daniel's heart.

One night the king had a strange dream. He called for all his wise men to tell him what the dream was and what it meant. None of the men knew what the dream was about, so the king ordered them to be killed.

Daniel asked if he could talk to the king. He told the king what the dream meant. He also told the king that he knew the secret of the dream not because he was greater or wiser than the other men. He said it was because God wanted them to live. The king spared the lives of all the wise men, including Daniel and his friends. Daniel did not brag about his gifts, or how great he was. He just talked about God's greatness and goodness. He was humble.

A SERVANT

God helped Daniel climb the mountains because he was a servant to the king. It did not matter if the king was evil and wicked. When you want to help and serve others, even if they are not nice, it is like getting under them and lifting them up. God, your Father, sees what you are doing. He will come and lift you up as you are serving others. God will bless you as He changes the hearts of those you serve. That is why Jesus said, "*If anyone wants to be first, he shall be last of all and servant of all*" (Mark 9:35).

ANOTHER DREAM

The king had another dream. It was about how the king would be punished for being so evil. Once again Daniel knew what the dream was about and who it was for. Was Daniel glad that the king was going to be punished and get what he deserved? No way! Daniel was sad about the dream. He wished it was for the king's enemies, instead. Daniel was loyal to the king. That meant he only wanted the best for his leader. Daniel honored the king not because he was good or bad. He honored the king because he honored God, and his royal mission.

CLIMBING TO THE TOP

Daniel was God's special agent, just like you. He was able to come into the enemy's kingdom of darkness. When he became a servant of the king, God's light was turned on, and darkness left. The king's sinful heart changed. He said, "I praise and honor the King of Heaven, who is true and just!" (see Daniel 4:37). The king was saved! The most evil kingdom was touched by Heaven! An entire nation turned to God! Satan lost because Daniel climbed to the top of the mountain!

GATHER YOUR STUFF

If you were going to go on a hike in the woods, you would get ready by gathering all the things you were going to need. You would then pack them in a sack, or backpack. So, what are you going to take for your journey to the mountains, to the different parts of your life? What will go into your backpack? What has your Papa given you for this exciting adventure?

Keys of Power and Authority: This is the trophy and prize Jesus won for you. As a royal ruler, you have Father God's power and authority.

Faith Eyes: These are the eyes of your heart. You will be able to see the "unseen" worlds of God's Kingdom, and the kingdom of darkness. You will also see what the Father is doing in Heaven, just like Jesus did.

Prayer: This is like bringing "lightning" down from Heaven. It will let loose the good things from Heaven, and tie up the bad things that are on earth.

Grace: This is God's promise to give you all the help you will need to complete your royal mission.

God's Presence: You will have the promise of the Father's love, peace, courage, and protection. The strength of His joy will be a great help. With God's presence you will have no fear of the enemy, or what people think.

A Mirror: God will show you that you are just like His Son, Jesus. You are more than a winner. You have His glory and power.

Angels: As you speak the same words that are in the Father's heart, angels will rise up to help bring Heaven to earth.

God Stories: Sharing stories about God's love and power will do amazing things. It will open people's hearts, and make them hungry for the Father's goodness.

Not only do you have all these great things to take along on your mission, but you also have a Guide, a best Friend, the *Holy Spirit*.

You will be "smeared" with the anointing of the Holy Spirit. God's power and love will "rub off" on people you touch.

You will "leak" the Holy Spirit wherever you go. His presence and power will flow out of you to do "impossible" things, like miracles. These signs and wonders will point the way to God's love and goodness.

You will get to be filled, and refilled with God's love and joy. As you soak in His presence, it will be like getting a drink of cool water. This will help you stay fresh and strong on your journey.

Your spirit will speak in tongues. It is your special language to God. It will bless Him, and make your spirit grow stronger each day.

YOUR BACKPACK

As you can see, you have been given so many amazing and wonderful things to pack into your backpack. But what about the backpack? It is special too, if it is going to carry all those great gifts and promises.

Your backpack is your heart, and is one of the most important things to take with you to complete your royal mission.

Daniel had the perfect heart, or backpack. His heart:

- Was humble. He gave God all the glory for the things that happened.
- Wanted to serve God, and the king.
- Was loyal to the king, even if the ruler was evil.
- Honored the king, because he honored God.
- Was trusted by the king.

If your backpack, or heart, is like Daniel's, if you are willing to serve and give away what God has given you, then you will reach the mountain tops of your life wherever you go.

On the mountain tops:

- God's Kingdom will come.
- Heaven will touch earth.
- The enemy's kingdom of darkness will fall.
- Nothing will be impossible.
- People's lives and places will change.
- Revival will happen!

- You will complete your royal mission

Let the journey begin!

TIME WITH YOUR KING

This is going to be a very special time with your Papa.

Begin by saying, "I love you, Papa."

Climb into His lap, and just rest in His arms. Listen to what He says.

He will tell you again how much He loves you.

You will feel special. You will feel rich.

Tell your Father how happy you are to be one of His children, one of His royal rulers.

Let Him know you want His Kingdom to come.

Tell Him you want to show His love and power to others wherever you go.

Ask Papa God to show you the mountains, the different parts of your life.

He will show you what they are.

You will see your home, school, church, and where you play.

Open your heart. Let your Father show you what He has given you for your royal mission.

Thank Him for each one.

Thank your Guide and Friend, the Holy Spirit.

Ask the Father to touch your heart, your backpack.

Ask Him for the heart of Daniel.

He will give you a heart to serve, honor, and help others even if they are not nice.

God will touch their hearts, as you show them His love.

Thank your heavenly Father for this special time.

JOURNAL TIME

Write about what your Father showed you and gave you.

_____

_____

_____

_____

_____

What mountains of your life did you see?

_____

_____

_____

_____

_____

Write and draw what you saw in your heart.

_____

_____

_____

_____

_____

_____

_____

_____

_____

What is your heart, or backpack, like?

_____

_____

_____

_____

_____

_____

_____

Is it like Daniel's?

_____

_____

_____

_____

_____

_____

_____

Did God show you any people He wants you to serve and help? Write their names.

_____

_____

_____

_____

_____

_____

Do you feel as if you can climb to the "top of the mountains"?

_____

_____

_____

_____

_____

_____

JOURNEY ADVENTURES

As your Father shows you the mountains, the different areas of your life:

Begin to pray for Heaven to come.

God will show you what to "let loose" from Heaven.

He will show you what to "tie up" on earth.

The Holy Spirit will lead you to people you can help and serve.

He will give you pictures and words about them.

They will be words that will help them.

It will make them feel special.

They will feel that God is not angry at them.

They will feel God loves them, and that He is not far away.

Don't be shy. Let the Holy Spirit help you.

Write what happened when you told them the nice things that God said about them.

_____

_____

_____

_____

_____

_____

_____

_____

_____

_____

_____

_____

_____

_____

Be willing to give away what God has given you.

Write about the miracles that happened when you prayed for people.

_____

_____

_____

_____

_____

_____

_____

_____

_____

_____

_____

_____

Write about how people are changing.

Write about how the mountains are changing in your life.

Be like Daniel and thank God for everything that happens.

TIME WITH YOUR KING

Write about what your Father shows you.

LEADER'S GUIDE...

...is comprised of 12 lessons (one for each brochure) and can be used for a quarterly curriculum, home-school, or devotions.

The Leader's Guide comes in a 3-ring binder. Each lesson contains a memory verse, a note to the teacher, materials needed list, and lots of fun ideas. *A complete set of the brochures are included with each Leader's Guide.*

BROCHURES

Each brochure is designed to bring children into a closer relationship and better understanding of "Papa" God. Because they are simply stated & visually appealing it is easy for a teacher, or parent to get children interested and involved. Please visit our website for a brief description of each brochure. Topics Include:

WHAT WAS GOD THINKING WHEN HE MADE YOU?

4 KEYS TO BRING HEAVEN TO EARTH

STEPS TO PRAYING FOR HEALING

GOD HAS NICE THINGS TO SAY

SOAKING IN GOD'S PRESENCE

VISITING HEAVENLY PLACES

GOD IS IN A GOOD MOOD

2 DOORS TO FREEDOM

GOD'S HEALING LOVE

PRAYER MAPPING

INTERCESSION

JOURNALING

God's Bucket of Love is ten short exercises to help children receive and experience the Father's Love. This book can be used with the leader's guide. 8 ½ x 11

My Heart is a Bucket is ten short exercises to help children invite God's presence and hear His voice This book can be used with the leader's guide. 8 ½ x 11

"SOAKING" CD

Our Heavenly Father loves us so much that He wants us to be filled and refreshed with His presence every day!"

An unique children's ministry resource that combines a short teaching segment with an invitation for God's very presence to personally "soak" the seed that was placed into the children's hearts. (CD includes instrumental music for "soaking" time).